THE
RABBIT COOK

J. C. Jeremy Hobson and Philip Watts

THE CROWOOD PRESS

First published in 2010 by
The Crowood Press Ltd
Ramsbury, Marlborough
Wiltshire SN8 2HR

www.crowood.com

British Library Cataloguing-in-Publication Data
A catalogue record for this book is available from the British Library.

ISBN 978 1 84797 229 3

Originated by The Manila Typesetting Company

Printed and bound in India by Replika Press

Contents

Acknowledgements

Some of the recipes contained within these pages have been adapted by us and are based on classically traditional ideas. A few come from Victorian (or older) books in our possession, and three or four first saw the light of day in our book *Cook Game*, also published by The Crowood Press. A great proportion of the recipes have, however, come about as a result of the kindness shown to us by various chefs, cooks, game dealers and enthusiastic amateurs up and down the country, and we are indebted to all of them for their time and willingness to share their knowledge. It never ceases to amaze us just how readily people are prepared to make recipes public, which they have developed and may have taken hours to perfect.

In particular we'd like to thank (and in no order!) Richard Campbell; Kinga and Edd McArdle (Edd has also helped us with other books in the past); Kevin Kindland, head chef at The Boar's Head, Ripley, North Yorkshire; Ben Burston and his head chef Richard Bridgens at The Rising Sun, Milland, Liphook, Hampshire; Paul Whittome (owner), Andrew McPherson (director) and Gemma Arnold (chef) at The Hoste Arms, Burnham Market, Norfolk — thank you all for your superb hospitality, and thanks Gemma for coming in to cook the dishes on what should have been your day off! Thanks, too, to Simon Cadge, head chef at The Old Bridge, Huntingdon, and to Stuart Fry and Stephen Treadwell at The Bell at Horndon on the Hill, Essex. Chris and Alison Davy looked after us well at The Rose and Crown, Romaldkirk, Co. Durham, as did James Rogers at The Dog at Grundisburgh, Suffolk. Thanks to Lawrence and Julia Murphy at Fat Olives, Emsworth, Hampshire; Mariangela Karlovitch of the Medura Resort Hotel, Naxos, Greece, and to Tricia Watts for her rosti recipe!

As pickles and chutneys go so well with a good many rabbit dishes, we have included a few recipes from our book *Making Traditional and Modern Chutneys, Pickles and Relishes* and therefore would like to thank Mary Hart, Lynn Brodie and Anne Lambert for allowing us to use them here.

'Contacts' are an essential part of any research: mercifully we seem to be blessed with more than our fair share, to all of whom we are truly grateful. Again in no particular order, we would like to thank Chris Hinchliffe for her sterling recipe research on our behalf; Steve Chesnutt, general manager at The Boar's Head, Ripley, North Yorkshire; Sir Thomas and Lady Ingilby, owners of the aforesaid establishment; John Hoskins, owner of The Old Bridge, Huntingdon and his general manager, Nina Beamond; Joanne Butler at The Bell at Horndon on the Hill; and last, but certainly not least, Naomi Roberts, PR and Promotions Executive at Bonner & Hindley Communications, Leeds. Naomi did a brilliant job of organizing a 'road trip' taking in several of the fine inns and hotels that are associated with the Great Inns of Britain scheme, fully explained later in this book.

Incidental photographs are often hard to come by, but we struck lucky in Norfolk when we dropped into J. & D. Papworth (Butchers and Graziers) at their Swaffham shop, where we were given *carte blanche* to photograph whatever we thought to be of interest on the counter display. Similarly, having had an hour to spare when in the North of England, we rang Stephen and Alison Morrell of Teesdale Game at Barnard Castle on the off chance that they might be able to help with a couple of 'filler' photos we were after – they could and they did, but not only that, they were kind enough to offer us a copy of *their* recipe book, written in collaboration with professional author Malcolm L. Pearce. The book was part of Malcolm's *The Easy Cook* series and entitled *The Game and Cheese Book*. In it were some superb ideas and recipes, and so we subsequently wrote to Alison, Stephen and Malcolm requesting permission to include some in *The Rabbit Cook*. Permission was kindly granted, for which thanks are offered. The recipe for 'Fennel and Borlotti Bean Bake' was taken from *The Olive Oil Cookbook* by Louise Pickford (Salamader, 1994).

There is at least one other to acknowledge as having been kind enough to assist in compiling *The Rabbit Cook*: Oliver Bone is the curator of The Ancient House Museum of Thetford Life where we found some interesting facts and photographs appertaining to warrening and the history of rabbit keeping throughout the ages.

Finally, whilst making every effort to ensure that the recipes included in this book have been cleared for copyright, there is no absolute guarantee that recipes accepted in good faith from people keen to help with our project have not been adapted from recipes that have already previously appeared in books or on the internet. Therefore, should anyone reading this book feel that their own recipes, or a part of them, have been taken without permission, we can only offer our sincere apologies and promise that, if they were to get in touch with us via the publishers, we will make suitable amends in future reprints.

Introduction

From our experiences it seems that you only have to mention the fact that you are writing a rabbit cook book and you will be inundated with ideas and suggestions – a fact for which we are, of course, extremely grateful.

Although rabbit pie is generally thought of as being a traditional rural dish, evoking memories of the British countryside when the sun always shone and ruddy-faced farm workers rested against a cornstook during a break from the rigours of harvest, rabbit meat is also a major component of many European recipes. Long enjoyed by Mediterranean land workers, the wild rabbit appears in countless Greek, Spanish and Italian recipes – and not just as a basic stomach filler, but also as a refined and quite exotic dish to be set on the high table of any influential gathering. Likewise, there are few rural French dwellers who do not still keep a hutch or two of rabbits destined for the Sunday dinner table. In fact, because of their ease of keeping and quick maturity, we have decided not to shirk the possibly emotive issue of breeding and keeping rabbits for the table, and subsequently offer a little advice on doing so in the final chapter.

In the UK, whilst there is sometimes an element of doubt on the part of the modern-day household cook as how best to prepare and serve a rabbit (wild or shop-bought), our predecessors have been doing so for generations – indeed centuries – and it is time that this most excellent meat source is well and truly brought back into vogue. With the recipes included here, we feel there is no doubt that the unsure will be reassured, and having tried one or two, will be left wondering what they were nervous about!

Once the basic principles have been mastered, the only limitation to creating a marvellous and completely unique dish is your imagination. As an example, someone told us of a recipe where the rabbit was cooked in champagne – a conversation which then resulted in much discussion as to whether it was essential to use expensive champagne or whether a cheap sparkling wine or cava wouldn't do equally as well. It was finally decided that it would, and the resultant recipe appears on page 65. That's the great thing about cooking: classic recipes can be adapted, and new ones invented. Many of those that appear here are variations on a theme and are delightful examples of an individual's imagination, as well as being a clever use of local produce used to accompany the main ingredient.

Although not classed as 'game', wild rabbits do, however, tend to come into their own during the late summer and autumn in much the same way as the season's pheasant and partridge. Young ones will be mature but tender – taking only a few minutes of pan-frying to produce a succulent and simple dish – and all will be in good condition owing to the bountiful abundance of natural food to be found at that time. Make the most of it and create rabbit-based recipes that include orchard fruits, wild damsons and blackberries – for some fortunate reason, most types of game dishes can be enhanced even further by using such ingredients.

And don't forget the less obvious either: young nettles, for instance, are similar to spinach when cooked, and their inclusion as an accompaniment will perhaps cause a little start of surprise on the part of your supper guests, and will most certainly prove to be a talking point. As winter approaches, the vegetable garden can provide the perfect accompaniments to many of the recipes included here, and will help ignite the warm glow of satisfaction that comes from being a true hunter gatherer.

Finally, we make no apologies for including half a dozen recipes that first appeared in our book *Cook Game* (The Crowood Press, 2007): they are far too good not to pass on to new readers, and if you were kind enough to have already bought a copy of *Cook Game* then worry not – there are, contained within these pages, many more completely new recipes for you to try!

J. C. Jeremy Hobson
Philip Watts
Summer 2010

Jeremy Hobson (left) and Philip Watts preparing for another photo session!

Getting Started

Without the humble rabbit, many country folk would have fared far less well than they did in times of poverty and war. Irrespective of whether or not it was sourced legitimately or illegally by poaching, it has been a staple of the rural diet for nearly 1,000 years, and it was probably only when the viral disease myxomatosis first appeared in the 1950s that rabbit meat began to be eaten less regularly. It is, however, nowadays once more enjoyed by a great many people, especially those who participate in field sports and for whom the 'chase' is a vital part of bringing fresh meat to the table.

FIRST CATCH YOUR RABBIT!

Although we don't need to go into too much detail in what is essentially a recipe and cookery book, it is nevertheless useful to, as Mrs Beeton famously said, first catch your hare – or in this case, rabbit! (As a point of interest regarding this oft-quoted saying, although it is commonly used, it is, in fact, not only misquoted, but also misattributed! The original *bon mot* began life as 'Take your hare when it is cased', and according to *The Oxford Dictionary of Quotations*, it was not written by Mrs Beeton at all!)

Shooting

Shooting rabbits with a shotgun after they have been flushed from rough undergrowth by spaniels has long been considered a 'gentleman's' sport. Enjoyed for the skill of shooting rather than as a means of obtaining meat for the kitchen, any rabbits shot would most likely have been given to the cook in order that she could make a cheap meal for the indoor staff, or even to the gamekeeper to be boiled up as dog food, or as part of a secret protein-based concoction fed to his game-bird chicks. Nowadays, though, rabbits are an important and exciting element of a day's rough shooting for anyone who enjoys a little countryside sport. Rabbits are normally shot at short range, so the most 'open' of game guns are ideally suited to rabbit shooting. A 28g load of no. 6 shot is generally accepted as being the best cartridge.

Some places, naturally, are better than others for rabbit shooting. Favoured spots include small fields bordered by woods, brush and briars; along drainages and fencerows where vegetation has grown up; in recently cleaned timber clear-fell; in brushpiles; and in densely covered power-line tracks. The rabbit's favourite cover includes blackberry patches, briars, honeysuckle, thick grass and weeds, and even rolled hay bales, abandoned farm machinery, irrigation pipes and culverts.

Rough-shooting methods vary, but one of the best ways is to enter a likely place and begin walking through it very slowly: go ten paces, then stop for about thirty seconds, then repeat the process. The sound of the approach may flush some rabbits, but very often it is the period when you pause that causes the rabbit to panic and bolt. When shooting with others, walk in line and about twenty paces apart. Rabbits in heavy cover seldom offer more than an instant in which you can make your shot, and so you will have to be a proficient snap-shooter: see the rabbit, check that it's a safe shot, shoulder the gun and shoot – all in one fluid movement!

Stalking with Air Rifles

As well as shotgun shooting, there is of course the more subtle art of stalking rabbits with an air rifle. There are many rifles on the market that are more than suitable for shooting rabbits, but there are basically two types. First, recoiling rifles powered by an internal spring, which is compressed by either cocking the action via a break-barrel or under-lever; second, pre-charged pneumatic types operated by compressed air. These rifles are generally available without a licence, and from the age of fourteen you can shoot an airgun on your own, and without adult supervision, provided you are on private land and have the consent of the landowner – but check current law by contacting the British Association for Conservation and Shooting (BASC). A telescopic sight is an almost obligatory addition if one has to have any hope of killing cleanly and efficiently. Quality ammunition is also essential. Again, expert thinking is that a standard dome head-type pellet is best for both accuracy and efficiency.

Rabbit shooting with a rifle of any kind requires patience and accuracy.

Since obviously you need to get particularly close to rabbits when using an air rifle, clothing of subdued colour will be required. Camouflaged gear breaks up a person's overall outline, making it more difficult to be seen by the rabbits. However, no amount of specialist clothing will prevent you from being scented by your quarry should you approach from the wrong direction. The general rule of any form of stalking (or indeed for that matter, photography or general wildlife observation) is that you should keep away from any exposed areas or skyline, and that a stalk should be conducted with the wind direction coming towards, rather than away from you.

Ferreting and Long-Netting

The use of ferrets for rabbiting is a technique devised by the Romans. In England, the tradition of rabbit hunting with ferrets goes back to a law created in 1390, which restricted the ownership of ferrets only to those with an income greater than 40s per year. This was to prevent the working classes from using them to poach rabbits – which is somewhat bizarre, as in recent years, ferrets have always had a working man's image.

The basic principles are very simple: it is a matter of approaching the rabbit bury quietly, covering any obvious holes with small purse nets (secured by a peg) that draw up and enclose the rabbit as it bolts, and releasing a ferret down the hole. In times gone by, the ferrets were muzzled in order to prevent them from killing a rabbit and feeding from it, but this practice is not much used nowadays. Sometimes a light cord line was attached

The result of a successful foray after rabbits.

to a small collar around another ferret's neck (usually a male or 'hob') and in this way non-muzzled ferrets that had killed underground and holed up could be located and dug down to by means of working out how much cord had been paid out.

Modern ferreters are more likely to use an electronic beeper attached to a collar, the exact location of where the ferret is underground then being transmitted to a receiver held in the hand of the ferret's owner as he patiently stands and waits. Once a rabbit does bolt, it is a question of getting hold of it quickly and dispatching it by either 'chinning' it (see below) or breaking its neck in the following fashion: take the rabbit's back legs in one hand and encompass its neck with the other before stretching the neck and simultaniously pulling back, in the same way as one would wring the neck of a chicken. Some ferreters and countrymen advocate the use of a karate chop at the back of the neck, but this is not easy to do effectively and could cause unnecessary suffering.

Long-netting is a complicated business, and it requires considerable skill to correctly set fine-meshed nets that may be many metres in length and about a metre (39in) in height. The nets are supported by light stakes, normally of hazel that have been cut previously from the woods or hedgerows. Often carried out at night, long-netting was a method much loved by poachers, the idea being to quickly and quietly set out the necessary lengths of net between where rabbits were known to be grazing and their burrows. Once the net has been erected, the rabbits are gently driven homewards and caught in the soft folds of netting as they do so. Once a rabbit hits the net, the people standing by have to work swiftly in order to dispatch one and then another in fast succession. The favoured method of doing this has always been to 'chin' the rabbit by placing one hand round the neck; putting the palm of your other hand under the chin and pushing the head back.

Mooching

The term 'mooching' loosely describes either someone wandering aimlessly and with no set purpose, or to poke about looking for something for nothing. Whilst these are not exact dictionary definitions, they are close enough to serve to explain the way a countryside 'mooch' might have ended up with a rabbit for the pot!

Although not really a specific means of catching and killing rabbits, mooching has always been synonymous with poaching and there is many a tale of poachers who could walk innocently along the road whilst their dog quietly hunted the field-side of a hedgerow unseen by casual onlookers, the gamekeeper or the farmer. Some of these dogs were apparently so skilled at their job that they would hunt, kill and carry a rabbit to the next gateway or gap and deliver it to its owner, who would then slip it into the concealed pocket on the inside of his jacket. Occasionally these dogs were so good that they would lie quietly out of sight if they heard their owner talking to someone they'd happened to encounter whilst walking down the road. Nowadays great care must be taken not to fall foul of the current Hunting Act when using any dogs to hunt rabbits (or hares).

Sometimes it is possible to catch a squatting rabbit whilst out on a quiet country walk. One of the authors managed it just the once by spotting a rabbit and avoiding eye contact whilst appearing to walk past. A quick sideways grab between the bottom of the ribcage and the top of the haunches meant that the rabbit could be picked up and killed without being scratched by its quite powerful back legs and very sharp claws.

Hours spent in generally mooching about on land where you have permission to shoot or ferret is always useful: time spent in recognizance is never wasted, and will help in ensuring that your sport is more likely to be successful, with rabbits brought home for the table. Of course if you have not the time, inclination or opportunities to catch your own, there may be no option but to procure your main cooking ingredient from a commercial source!

Game Dealers, Butchers, Farmers' Markets and Elsewhere

Although not often seen in British supermarkets, wild rabbits are often on sale at high class butchers and farmers' markets – and of course, from game dealers whose contact details can often be found in *Yellow Pages*, on the internet or even in various local food booklets from the nearest tourist board office. Wild rabbit meat, which is leaner and tastier than the farmed variety, has a fabulous, subtle, gamey flavour and despite being available for most of the year, comes into its own from July to December. It is also available by mail order from a number of suppliers – again a web search will provide all you need to know.

When buying from a butcher's or game dealer's, you will possibly have the choice of whether to buy a rabbit in the fur, or skinned and ready for the oven. Whichever way they are bought, they should be large enough to yield a decent amount of meat, but not so large as to suggest that they might be too old to be tender – wild rabbits weighing much more than a kilo (2¼ lb) should only be cooked in a slow-cook casserole. Younger, smaller animals will be better

A good traditional butcher's such as this will provide you with not only farmed meats, but also rabbits and game in season.

suited to quick-cook methods such as roasting or barbecuing. Sometimes the purveyor will use the term 'fryer' to refer to a young rabbit and a 'roaster' to denote a mature animal. The quality of young rabbits bought in the fur can be further determined by ears that tear easily and the bones of the lower jaw, which break easily with a little pressure. The interior of the animal should smell fresh and sweet with no pronounced gamey smell. Kidneys well covered with fat are another sign of good condition, and overall the body should be plump and well fleshed. Traditionalists say that a young female rabbit is always better than the male, especially near the start of the breeding season when the flesh of the male tends to become rank and stronger in flavour – but sexing your rabbit is generally beyond the remit of most sellers!

PREPARING YOUR RABBIT

Paunching
A wild rabbit will have had its intestines removed (paunched) as soon as it has been killed. It is usually done in the field for two reasons; first and most importantly, leaving the innards in for any length of time will taint the meat and spoil it, but second, it's much easier to leave the paunch to rot down and be 'recycled' in the countryside than to put up with the smell in the dustbin at home! If you are the one responsible for catching and killing the rabbit, you might like to empty its bladder before you paunch it: should you cut or catch a full bladder whilst paunching, the contents are quite likely to taint the meat. To do this, pick the rabbit up and hold it vertically with its head towards you and its belly uppermost. Put your hand around its nether regions, and give the area below the ribcage a squeeze with your thumb. Push your thumb downwards towards the rear end in order to expel any urine that's still contained in the bladder.

To paunch the rabbit, turn it on to its back and feel along the centre of the ribs for the loose fur and skin; pull this up and away from the centre by pinching it with your finger/thumb. The loose flap of skin can then be pulled up and slit with a sharp knife. Very carefully make a slit from between the rabbit's back legs right up to the breast bone; at this stage, do not cut too deeply or you will pierce the innards. If done correctly, you should have cut through the skin and left the inner flesh exposed; then with the point of your knife, carefully cut through the flesh of the belly to expose the guts. Next, reach in with your fingers and carefully remove the stomach, intestines and urinary tract; however, keep the liver and kidneys as these might be quite desirable in your intended recipe.

Skinning
Once you are back at home, you can skin and joint the rabbit. In the interests of domestic harmony it might be better to do this outside or in the garden shed, but it's probably easiest on the kitchen work surface. Wherever is chosen, the job should be carried out on an impervious surface or one protected by polythene – it is best not to use newspaper as the print can get on to the meat.

With the rabbit on its back and its head towards you, start to separate the skin from the meat, all the time working around the body from both sides until you have completely separated the meat from the skin. Put your left hand under the skin and grip the rabbit; using the other hand, it should be quite easy to peel off the rest of the skin.

You will find that it is still attached at the head, legs and tail, but these can be removed with a pair of secateurs or a sharp knife. Be very careful in doing this, because unless you remove the legs at the joint, the bones will be very sharp. The head is best removed by cutting round the neck with a sharp knife, then dislocating the vertebrae with a twisting motion. Now wash your rabbit to remove any blood and debris that is sticking to it. Take particular care to ensure that all the area around the rectum has been cleared away. Dry the carcass by using kitchen paper or a cloth. Some recipes call for a whole rabbit to be used, in which case your work is done; others may call for a rabbit to be jointed.

Jointing

Place your washed and dried rabbit on a chopping board. To joint your rabbit, cut off the front legs by using a sharp knife inserted between the muscles that join the legs to the hips and shoulders; then cut through the bone at the joint with a strong knife – if you can pinpoint the exact place where the bone joint is, it is a very easy procedure.

The saddle joint is next. Again, the saddle is most easily jointed by inserting a knife between the vertebrae rather than trying to hack through randomly. If you intend doing much jointing and preparation, it may pay to invest in a butcher's cleaver, as with that, you can chop through at almost any point. So far you should have two front legs and a saddle joint. Now take what remains of the rear half and lay it on your board belly up. Run the knife round the area just in front of the rear legs and remove each one by means of a

Rabbits in various stages of preparation.

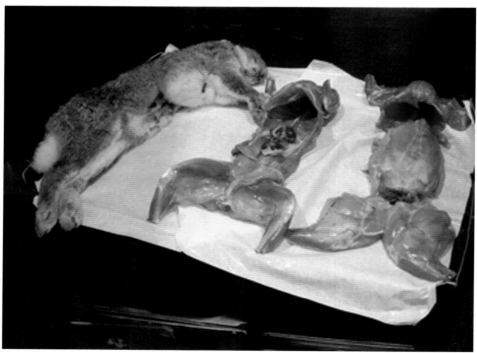

twisting motion. You should end up with five pieces of very useable rabbit, together with what remains of the carcass from having removed the back legs (and also the ribcage and lower neck), which will prove invaluable in creating an excellent stock.

Soaking

Whether or not to soak the rabbit pieces overnight in cold, salted water (add a tablespoon of salt) is often a cause of disagreement among some rabbit-eating *aficionados*. Some do, and some don't: doing so does tend to make the meat look paler, but more importantly, it acts as a sort of marinade that breaks down some of the meat tissues. You could, however, use any marinade you liked, or as directed in a particular recipe. Generally though, young rabbits can be cooked exactly as they are.

STORING AND FREEZING

Whilst fresh rabbit will keep in the fridge for several days, great care must be taken in preparing them for the freezer if one is to avoid the possibility of the meat suffering from freezer burn and becoming too dry. For this reason it might be worth considering cooking whatever recipe has been chosen, and freezing it once it is cooked. Laziness may tempt you into freezing freshly shot or ferreted rabbits whilst still in the fur – however don't – it is bad practice, and the meat will suffer due to air being trapped in the fur.

It is important to have an organized freezer where everything is instantly accessible. An untidy heap of badly labelled and poorly stored joints can result in those at the very bottom never getting used and eventually being thrown away due to becoming 'out of date', or succumbing to the effects of freezer burn. Rabbit meat kept for too long may remain useable, but it certainly tends to lose some of its flavour, and none should be kept frozen for more than twelve months at the very outside. Within each tray, try and ensure that the bags with the oldest labelled dates are placed to the top so that their contents are always the first to be used, and ensure that any sharp or protruding bones do not puncture the bag in which they are wrapped by wrapping them in kitchen foil. It is also important to make sure that all air is excluded from the bag by the simple expedient of inserting a drinking straw into the almost closed neck of the polythene bag and sucking it out.

Remember that a full freezer operates far more efficiently than one that is only partially full, and if necessary, fill any gaps in the freezer with newspapers.

COOKING UTENSILS

All jobs are made easier with the right tools, and bringing good quality food to the table is no exception. As well as the obvious pots and pans and an assortment of mixing bowls, at some stage you will require two or three wooden spatulas (not metal, in case they damage the inner surfaces of your pans), as well as some ladles and spoons – both solid and slotted. As far as pans are concerned, look for heavy stainless steel, anodized aluminium or enamel-coated cast-iron models that allow even heat distribution and prevent burning. Copper is an excellent heat conductor, but it is a little more expensive and requires maintenance – most copper cookware is lined with tin, and over time the lining will need to be resurfaced. Have a selection of pans that include a variety of different sized saucepans, skillets, a stockpot and a roasting pan.

Buy a colander that has secure handles – the cheapest often have ones that are riveted through soft metal and will pull out at the earliest opportunity. Although whisking and beating can be done with a kitchen fork, a whisk will make the creation of sauces that much easier. Use a skimmer for removing surplus fat from a casserole or pot-roast, and a funnel for returning unused oil back to the bottle. A vegetable peeler is easier to use than a knife, but better still, try to get away with gently scrubbing vegetables rather than peeling them, as to do so removes essential nutrients found in their skins.

It's a shame that the giving of knives has long been considered to be unlucky (it being traditionally thought that doing so as a gift to a friend will sever the relationship) as good kitchen knives are an expensive item, and as such would make the perfect present for the rabbit cook. (Fortunately it is possible to overcome this problem if the giver includes a coin with the knife and which the receiver returns as 'payment'!) Good knives are absolute essentials in the kitchen. Look for high-carbon steel and a handle that fits nicely in your hand, and try to make sure that you eventually build up a collection that includes knives suitable for paring, boning and carving. Kitchen shears are also invaluable for jointing a rabbit carcass (as is a small butcher's cleaver), and a sharpening tool will hopefully ensure that a good blade is kept, and that your knives will never be, to use an expression of my grandfather's, 'So blunt that I could ride bare-bottomed to London on the edge and never do myself a mischief!'

USEFUL KITCHEN UTENSILS

A variety of saucepans/a roasting tin/vegetable steamer
Two sets of heavy-gauge stainless steel measuring spoons
Two glass liquid measuring jugs
Two chopping boards, one for meat, the other for vegetables
'Pyrex'-type mixing bowls
An assortment of non-scratch spatulas
Ditto good quality knives/vegetable peeler
Soup ladle/slotted spoons/wooden spoons
Kitchen tongs
Long-handled fork
Four-sided grater
Colander
Hard rubber whisk
Baster/meat thermometer/oven thermometer
Funnels and strainers
Black pepper grinder/garlic press
Can opener
Wooden skewers

Finally, equip your kitchen with a plentiful supply of kitchen roll, tinfoil, baking parchment, clingfilm and freezer storage bags, all of which will be in frequent use.

INGREDIENTS

Ingredients should be as fresh as possible – even those that have a shelf life such as dried spices and flour, because no matter what the food, it will in time go stale or deteriorate. With this in mind it pays to keep an eye on your store cupboards and to throw away anything that is seriously beyond its use-by date. It is, of course, possible to avoid such a situation by the simple expedient of making sure that every time you cook you use the older ingredients first, and that when you shop, you position the fresh ingredients *behind* the old. When you do go shopping, avoid over-stocking: just because a few items are on special offer there are no savings to be made if you eventually have to dispose of them.

More obviously, it is important to store vegetables carefully, and a suitable rack placed in a dark but airy corner is possibly the best thing for the job if you are not to be forever throwing away potatoes and carrots that have gone soft and soggy before you get the opportunity to use them. Much depends on their provenance: good quality local produce will undoubtedly last longer than vegetables that have flown thousands of miles and been kept in cold storage in various stages of 'rest' – but even so, a proper rack will pay dividends. Some vegetables are staple ingredients of many rabbit recipes found within this book; onions and garlic, for example, feature in many, as do mushrooms and fresh herbs.

STOREROOM ESSENTIALS

Good quality olive oil
Dijon mustard
Black pepper
Balsamic vinegar
Tinned beans
Tinned soups (those such as
    mushroom, for example, make
    a sauce or casserole base)
Flour

Rice
Vegetable oil
Red wine vinegar
Sea salt
Red wine
Tinned tomatoes (useful in sauces
    and casseroles)
Pasta

Essential Perishables
Fresh herbs/bay leaves
Onions
Lemons

Mushrooms
Garlic
Root vegetables (potatoes, carrots)

Fridge Essentials
Butter
Cream

Chicken or game stock
Crème fraîche/plain yoghurt

Growing Some of Your Own Ingredients

In keeping with the ethos of rabbit meat being freshly sourced, you might want to consider growing vegetables and herbs in order that what you include in the various recipes is equally as well sourced. Some form of vegetable gardening is possible in almost any back garden, especially if

Onions feature as a base ingredients in many rabbit recipes.

space is fully utilized by the inclusion of cloches and garden frames. By planting early under cloches, you can be sure of the first crops of the season and also, at the other end of the year, the latest.

The first objectives of anyone intending to grow vegetables must be to improve the productivity of the soil, as you will be very fortunate indeed if your garden is already perfect for your needs. Alternatively, consider using the raised bed system, as they can be very useful in small areas, and because of the nature of their construction can be adapted to suit any size of available space as well as being built near the kitchen door – thus saving trips to the furthest end of the garden in driving rain.

Most small gardens have space for a few herbs, and even those without any garden at all can grow some in pots on a patio or in a windowbox. Herbs likely to be of most use to the game cook include basil, bay, chives, dill, fennel, garlic, mint, parsley, rosemary, sage, tarragon and thyme. Many herbs are Mediterranean in origin and therefore do well in a drained and sheltered location; some are half hardy and will need winter protection, whilst others, such as chives, die back in the autumn, but provided that they've been regularly fed and watered the previous summer, will reappear the following spring. You can try and keep them growing during the winter by potting up a clump and bringing it indoors.

A vegetable garden will provide a great variety of possible ingredients.

Ravishing Rabbit Recipes

National and regional dishes from all over the world reflect the fact that rabbit meat is very versatile and works well with those flavours often used in chicken dishes, such as mustard and cream (France), tomato and herbs (Italy) and chilli (South America). It can be cooked in every way imaginable: from simply fried over a hot flame, oven baked or roasted, and in stews, casseroles and pies. For the adventurous cook we have included some recipes that at first glance might seem a little daunting, but which are, nevertheless, well worth making the effort to try.

The main problem, however, is the fact that, whilst other countries seem to accept a rabbit carcass as being a provider of cheap and easily accessible meat, we in the UK, in the second decade of the twenty-first century, are, as a general rule, daunted by the prospect. This is strange, really, considering the fact that our grandparents and great grandparents looked upon the rabbit as being a part of their staple diet. Perhaps it has to do with the fact that they were used to seeing rabbits 'in the fur' and hanging from the hooks at their local butchers, whereas unless we have partners who shoot, or country-living friends and relatives who offer the occasional fresh animal, we hardly ever see a rabbit, and unless it is prepared oven-ready, would baulk at what is on offer. Even when we do see it so prepared, do we immediately know exactly what to do with it? And for the tyro, there is always the latent fear of the unknown: will a rabbit dish taste 'gamey'? Many enthusiasts insist that rabbit meat is similar to chicken, but in our opinion, a correctly prepared and beautifully cooked rabbit is second to none. These recipes will, we hope, go a long way towards proving this statement.

Note: All recipes serve four unless otherwise stated.

Chicken and Rabbit Casserole

The addition of chicken to this recipe 'dilutes' what might be, to some, the slightly too gamey flavour of an older rabbit; this makes it a suitable introduction for anyone who has never before tried a game-inspired dish of any description.

1 rabbit
2 chicken quarters
2 large carrots, scraped and chopped

2.4ltr/4 pints water
1 medium-sized leek, roughly chopped
2 chicken stock cubes

1kg/2lb of potatoes, peeled and
  chopped into chunks

2 tablespoons chicken gravy granules
Salt and pepper to season

In a pan, place the water and boil the chicken and rabbit until cooked through (if the rabbit is whole, this will obviously take longer to cook than will the chicken quarters). When both rabbit and chicken are cooked, remove from the water and allow to drain and cool. Save the water. Strip the meat from the bones, and discard the bones and any chicken skin.

In a deep casserole dish place a layer of leek, carrots and potatoes; add the meat and then the remainder of the vegetables. Pour over the stock derived from boiling the meat, and add more water if necessary. Cover the casserole tightly and cook for at least one hour at gas mark 5/375°C.

Next, crumble in the chicken stock cubes and gravy granules. Stir well and return to the oven for 10 minutes. Remove from the oven and stir again (thicken with cornflour and water if a thicker casserole is preferred), and season to taste.

Note: Although this casserole is commonly eaten straightaway, it will actually improve if left overnight and reheated thoroughly the following day.

Kinga McArdle's Hungarian Rabbit and Dumpling Recipe

Kinga's husband Edd has helped us enormously with the compilation of our various recipe books. Kinga says, 'This is a recipe that my mother used when I was growing up in Hungary. In Hungary there are places that will farm rabbit for food, so you can get some good meat if you are lucky enough to have access to such a place. The sauce has a strong taste, and as a child I have to admit I didn't like it, but it was always my father's favourite! Now I'm a bit older I do find it delicious, and understand why my father liked it so much.'

1 whole rabbit, jointed
Duck fat or lard
Stock – made up of:
1 carrot, 1 onion, a small handful of
  chopped parsley,

300ml/10fl oz water, a juniper berry, a
  good pinch of sugar, and 1 spoonful of
  white or brown vinegar
Mustard

Cook the stock (adding the sugar and the vinegar last) for 20–30 minutes. Let it cool before pouring half of the stock on to the cleaned rabbit pieces, from which as many ligaments on the muscle as possible have been removed. Let them rest in the stock for 24 hours, moving them around the bowl occasionally.

Rub the rabbit pieces in duck fat or lard, as well as rubbing a roasting pan with the duck fat. Half roast the rabbit pieces, covered, at 180°C/gas mark 4 for approximately half an hour.

When the dumplings are made and cooking (see below), take the rabbit out of the oven, add some vegetables from the original stock to the dish, and cook the rabbit for another 10–15 minutes.

To make the sauce, take the remaining vegetables from the stock and put them in the blender. Add some of the water from the stock together with a little mustard, and blend it together; pour it over the rabbit and dumplings to serve.

For the bread dumplings with sauce

'This is as my mother used to make it – don't worry too much about the exact measurement of milk as it does depend upon the consistency desired. It is important to make sure that the mixture is "loose",' says Kinga.

3 bread rolls
600ml/20fl oz milk
2 eggs beaten
Some flour for 'binding'

A sprig of parsley, chopped
Pinch of mustard powder
Salt

Take the bread rolls, cut them up and soak them in milk and add the eggs. Let the mixture rest until it is all 'mashable' and the hard bits have softened. If you find that the crusty parts are still too hard and too big, use a hand mixer and run it over the hard bits. Add as much flour as makes it easy to form several little balls. Add the finely chopped parsley, mustard and a pinch of salt.

Half fill a cooking pan with water, add salt and a little oil, and bring it to the boil. Once the water is boiling, place the dumpling balls into the pan. (Tip: to start with, put the spoon that you are using to put the balls into the water into the hot water first in order that the balls will easily slide off it when you place them into the pan.) Wait until they all come up to the top. Taste a part of one to check if they are ready. Put some butter over them and place them on a serving plate together with the rabbit, and pour sauce over both (as described above).

Kinga McArdle's Hungarian Rabbit and Dumpling.

Curried Rabbit

The basic cooking methods for this recipe are very similar to those for *Rabbit in Champagne* (see page 69). However, the addition of curry will obviously give this dish a very different flavour.

30g/1oz butter	1½ tablespoons plain flour
1 teaspoon oil	600ml/1 pint stock
1 rabbit, jointed	1 tablespoon sultanas
2 large onions, chopped	1 teaspoon chutney
1 large cooking apple, peeled, cored and chopped	1 teaspoon redcurrant jelly
1 tablespoon curry powder	Seasoning

Heat the butter and oil in a frying pan and fry the rabbit joints until golden; transfer them to a casserole dish. Add the chopped onion to the pan and fry until soft, and then sprinkle over the rabbit, together with the chopped apple.

Put the curry powder and flour into the frying pan and fry for 2 minutes. Add the stock gradually and bring to the boil; then incorporate all the remaining ingredients and pour into the casserole.

Cover and cook at gas mark 3/170°C for 1½–2 hours. Serve on a bed of long-grained rice.

BRAISED RABBIT JOINTS

Joints of rabbit, quarters or halves of game birds and similar, can be very successfully braised or pot-roasted. The meat is first of all browned with the aid of a little fat or oil and then placed on a bed of vegetables in a casserole dish or pan (which must have a tightly fitting lid). Rather than merely using chopped vegetables as a base, a French mix makes the dish a lot more interesting.

On a board, chop or slice two carrots, one large onion, two cloves of garlic, two large tomatoes (these can be omitted if, like many people, you or your guests are not fans of cooked tomatoes) and some parsley (with the stalk removed). Heat a tablespoon of olive oil in the pan, put in the onions, season with a little sea salt and freshly ground pepper, and sweat over a low heat before adding the remaining ingredients. Rest the meat on the French mix and add a splash of white wine or just enough stock to prevent burning. Cover the pan and cook very gently until the meat is done. Times will obviously vary depending on the joint of rabbit being used.

Mumbled Rabbit

When we came across this recipe we had to include it simply because of its name! Apparently it has to do with the action of cooking, as in, 'I'm going to mumble a rabbit today' – but quite how it came about we've no idea (possibly local dialect?). Wherever the name originates, it is known that somebody, somewhere has been mumbling rabbits since the late seventeenth century when this recipe was first recorded.

700g/1½lb rabbit meat, cut from the bone and into chunks	100g/3½oz butter
1 bunch mixed herbs, tied tightly together	1 onion, peeled and finely
3 eggs	chopped

In a boiling, salted pan of water, simmer the rabbit meat and herbs until the meat is cooked and tender. About 10 minutes before you think this point will arrive, drop the three eggs into the water to hardboil. Remove, run under cold water, shell the eggs and finely chop. Take out and get rid of the bunch of herbs and then, with a slotted spoon, remove all the pieces of rabbit meat but retain the cooking liquid. In a pan, melt the butter, add the onion and sauté. Add the rabbit pieces and stir in the chopped eggs, and cook for a few minutes more over a low heat.

In the seventeenth century, the cooking liquid would most likely have been mopped up by chunks of bread, but some more modern adaptations of this dish suggest that you cook a batch of pasta in it and serve it all in together.

Slow-Cooked Rabbit with White Bean Mash and Roast Vegetables

Kevin Kindland is the head chef at The Boar's Head, Ripley, near Harrogate, North Yorkshire. He was very generous with his time when we visited him in connection with both this book and *The Pigeon Cook* (also published by Crowood); so too was Steve Chesnutt, general manager, and Sir Thomas and Lady Ingilby, owners of both The Boar's Head and nearby Ripley Castle.

The Ingilby family has received visitors at Ripley Castle for 700 years. Some, like Oliver Cromwell, were highly unwelcome: the rebel general found himself held at pistol point by 'Trooper Jane' Ingilby in the castle library. The Boar's Head restaurant is featured in most of the best known food guides and is associated with the Great Inns of Britain, a collection of independent, historic and very stylish inns, an idea formulated by Sir Thomas himself (alongside Paul Whitthome, owner of The Hoste Arms, Downham Market, Norfolk – see their recipe for 'Assiette of Rabbit' on page 29).

200g/7oz haricot beans	2 carrots, cut into large diced pieces
1ltr/1¾fl oz vegetable stock	2 parsnips, cut into large diced pieces
10g/¼oz rosemary	16 button onions
Butter	4 loins of rabbit
1ltr/1¾pints chicken stock	Rabbit jus (rabbit bones, onions, carrot,
8 legs of rabbit	leeks, thyme and red wine cooked down to
Salt and pepper	a sauce)
Oil	Pea shoots

Slow-Cooked Rabbit with White Beans Mash and Roasted Vegetables.

Soak the beans in cold water the night before. Remove the beans and rinse off the water, then leave in fresh, clean water for half an hour. Then place in a pan with the vegetable stock and rosemary, and bring to the boil, cooking until the beans are soft. Drain and mash like mashed potato before adding a little butter to taste.

Bring the chicken stock to the boil. Heat a large frying pan; season the rabbit legs with salt and pepper. Add oil to the frying pan and seal the rabbit pieces until golden brown. Place the rabbit legs in the stock and cook on low for 3 hours or until tender.

Roast the carrots, parsnips and onions until soft.

Season the rabbit loins, heat a large frying pan with butter and oil, and pan roast.

To present, place the white bean mash in the centre of the plate with the legs on top, place the carrot, parsnips and onions around the side, and finish with the rabbit jus and pea shoots.

Stuffed Roast Rabbit

Relatively simple to prepare and make, the stuffing adds the fruitiness that goes together so well with many rabbit dishes, and in addition helps keep the meat moist.

1 whole rabbit
8 rashers of streaky bacon

2 tablespoons red wine

To make the stuffing

1 x 400g/14oz tin of apricots, chopped into small pieces	115g/4oz breadcrumbs
50g/1¾oz chopped walnuts	1 beaten egg
Juice of 1 orange (and a little grated rind)	Salt and black pepper

Place all the stuffing ingredients into a bowl and mix together well, then fill the rib cavity of the rabbit. Place in a roasting tin, lay over the bacon slices and cover loosely with tinfoil, and cook at gas mark 6/200°C for I hour.

Remove the foil and the bacon; baste the rabbit, roll the bacon slices and place all back in the roasting tin for a further 15 minutes. At the end of this time, add the wine to the resultant pan juices in order to make a thin gravy.

Serve with roast potatoes, red cabbage and cranberry sauce.

Rabbit Brawn

This is an old recipe that would have been made in many country cottages. If you remember your grandmother making brawn after the pig in the sty had been killed, this one's for you!

1 large rabbit, jointed	Blade of mace
2 pig's trotters	2 cloves
12 peppercorns	

Soak the rabbit in cold water (see 'Getting Started', page 15). Meanwhile, simmer the pig's trotters in water for 2 hours. Add the rabbit, peppercorns, mace and cloves, and simmer for a further 2 hours until the meat leaves the bones.

Cut the meat in pieces, and mix the rabbit and the meat from the trotters. Put into bowls and strain in the cooking liquid. Leave in a cold place to set (it will set because the gelatine in the trotters turns the stock into a type of jelly).

Keep in the refrigerator for up to three days, or cover and freeze.

Note: you could add a dash of vinegar to the water at the outset, as this will help to tenderize the meat – although with slow simmering as suggested, it will probably not be necessary.

Blackfriars Game Terrine

Cheating a little, given the book's title, this recipe uses not just rabbit, but all manner of game in season. It was devised and kindly given to us to publish by Andy Hook, the owner of Blackfriars Restaurant, Friars Street, Newcastle, which is, as far as can be established, the oldest purpose-built restaurant in the UK, with its origins dating back as far as 1239. Today Andy Hook and his team specialize in what he describes as 'classic but gutsy British food using fresh local and seasonal produce'. This particular recipe serves between four and eight people, according to Andy.

500g/1¼lb sausage meat
200g/7oz chopped liver
Freshly made breadcrumbs taken
  from two thick slices of bread
1 egg
1 handful of flat-leaf or curly parsley and
  thyme, chopped and mixed together
A few juniper berries
2 cloves garlic, chopped
1 'glug' red wine

1 'glug' brandy (optional)
Sea salt and black pepper
1kg/2¼lb game meat: pheasant, partridge,
  rabbit, pigeon, duck or even hare
A little olive oil (for frying the game meat)
1 small handful pistachio nuts, crushed
Diced and cooked carrots
1 handful gherkins
12 rashers of streaky bacon

Turn the oven to gas mark 2½/160°C. Mix together the sausage meat and liver, and add the breadcrumbs, egg, parsley, thyme, juniper berries and garlic. Add the red wine (and brandy if you want to be extravagant), and season with the sea salt and freshly ground black pepper. Mix thoroughly before turning out and rolling into a 'sausage' roughly the same length as your chosen terrine dish.

Next, chop and fry the game meat (in batches if necessary) in olive oil until golden brown. Mix in a bowl with the pistachios, cooked carrots and the handful of gherkins.

Line a terrine dish with the stretched rashers of streaky bacon, and add half the game meat mix; lay the forcemeat sausage down the middle, then heap on the remaining game mix. Fold the exposed strips of bacon over the top of the terrine and cover with kitchen foil and the terrine dish lid. Place the terrine dish in a roasting tin half-filled with hot water and cook in the oven for 1½ hours.

Press the terrine as it cools, with a block of snug-fitting wood and a couple of cans of baked beans, and leave overnight until completely cold. To serve the terrine: slice it thickly with a very sharp knife, place on a plate with a few dressed greens and some fruit chutney. Serve with hot toast.

The Rising Sun Rabbit Terrine

As their website claims, The Rising Sun in Milland, a village on the Hampshire/West Sussex borders, is:

> A true village local in the heart of unspoilt South Downs National Park countryside; renowned for its outstanding atmosphere, great food, Fullers ales, a long and varied wine list, and charming staff. Stylishly refurbished, spacious and light, and with vast gardens and terraces adorned with teak tables and parasols, this is a pub for all seasons and all occasions.

As I lived in the village for twenty years before moving to France, and Philip lives there now, we both know there is much substance to the claim! Ben Burston is the perfect 'mine host' and Richard Bridgens is head chef. Thanks to both for supplying the following recipe and photo opportunities.

Pack of pancetta, sliced
1 red onion
3 cloves garlic
3–4 sprigs thyme
225g/8oz pork sausagemeat

3 rabbits, de-boned and with the
    saddles removed and kept whole (put the
    saddles to one side)
115g/4oz frozen redcurrants
Pack of pancetta, sliced
Salt and pepper

Take a terrine dish and line with clingfilm. Then, overlapping them slightly, place strips of the pancetta all around the dish, including the bottom.

Finely chop the onion, garlic and thyme, and mix thoroughly with the sausagemeat. Mix in the strips of rabbit meat (excluding the saddles), season well, and throw in the redcurrants, mixing evenly. Place half of the mix into the terrine dish (it should come about half way to the top, says Richard), then lie the saddles in strips down the length of the terrine, placing the remaining mix over the top of this. Fold over the strips of pancetta so that the whole terrine is wrapped in it; then fold over the excess clingfilm, finally placing the lid over this.

Put the terrine dish in a *bain marie* or water bath half-filled with hot water, and cook for approximately 40 minutes at gas mark 3/170°C. To check it is cooked, probe the terrine (it should hold 68°C for at least 2 minutes). Rest well before slicing and serving.

The Rising Sun Rabbit Terrine.

Rabbit, Game and Mushroom Loaf

Sometimes a clear-out of the freezer brings forth a miscellaneous collection of game collected throughout the season. A game pie is the usual way of using up these 'odds and ends', but so too is this easily prepared recipe.

1 large Coburg loaf (or any crusty dome-shaped   1 beaten egg
    loaf baked in a similar fashion)
50g/1¾oz butter, melted

Remove the top from the loaf and cut out the soft, doughy bread from the base in order to create a bowl shape. Brush inside and out with the melted butter and then the beaten egg. Cook at gas mark 4/180°C for 8 minutes or until it looks golden brown.

For the filling
1 onion, finely chopped   1 tablespoon chopped mixed herbs
1 tablespoon flour   450g/1lb rabbit/game meat
200ml/7fl oz game stock   225g/8oz button mushrooms, sliced
Salt and pepper   A little butter (to sauté the mushrooms)
Pinch of mace

Fry the onion in the remainder of the melted butter, then add the flour and stir to a smooth paste. Add the stock, salt and pepper and quickly bring to the boil, then immediately reduce the heat and simmer for 3 or 4 minutes; remove the pan from the heat and add the mace and mixed herbs. Cut into shreds whatever game meat is being used, and add it to the sauce.

In another pan, sauté the mushrooms and place half of them in the bottom of the bread 'bowl'. Spoon over the filling mix, and cover this with the remainder of the mushrooms. Replace the 'lid' of the loaf and return to the oven to cook for a further 5 to 10 minutes.

Bring to the table complete, and carve the loaf as you would a normal everyday loaf – the filling should be quite firm and should stay in the slices rather than fall out in a heap! Serve with a salad, *mange tout* peas or French beans.

Assiette of Rabbit: Rack of Rabbit, Saddle of Rabbit, Confit of Leg Spring Roll, Sautéed Kidneys and Rabbit Liver Parfait

If you ever have cause to be in the Downham Market area of Norfolk, make a point of calling into The Hoste Arms, even if it is just for afternoon tea or a drink. Better still, try and engineer an overnight stay there. It is owned by Paul Whittome, co-founder of the hugely successful 'Great Inns of Britain' organization, and as such you can be sure of the freshest linen, the finest local produce and the friendliest staff.

'Great Inns of Britain' was formed in 1996, its aim being to create an alliance of premises offering first class, comfortable surroundings, great hospitality and even greater foods and wines at what one member calls 'honest prices'. Many of the inns and hotels

Assembling the rabbit parts in preparation for the 'Assiette of Rabbit' recipe.

involved have a strong interest in field sports, and some of them are able to arrange game fishing and shooting in the immediate vicinity. Others host lawn meets for the local hunt, and from what I've seen, all are situated in outstanding country locations.

Andrew McPherson joined Paul and The Hoste Arms in 1991 as their executive chef, and is now a director. He and his staff made us very welcome when we were on our travels in search of recipes for this book. Particular thanks are due to Gemma Arnold, who came in on her day off to prepare the recipes so that we could photograph them.

1 skinned and gutted rabbit
New potatoes

Prepare the rabbit by removing the legs, kidneys and liver. Cut out the saddle, and cook it by sealing it in a frying pan until slightly browned, then roasting it in the oven at gas mark 4/180°C for 12–15 minutes, taking care that it does not dry out; cook it on the bone, only removing the meat immediately prior to serving.

Cut out the racks (ribs), cleaning between the bones, and cook in the oven as before.

Finely slice new potatoes, blanch in salted boiling water until soft, and then fry in a little butter until golden. Gemma didn't specify the number of potatoes needed, no doubt thinking it a matter of personal taste and whether or not you are on a diet!

For the Confit of Leg Spring Roll

The rabbit legs

Duck fat

1 packet of filo pastry

1 banana shallot, finely diced

1 stick celery, finely diced

½ red pepper, finely diced

1 leek, finely diced

A little melted butter

On a slow heat, cover the rabbit legs with duck fat and cook until tender. Whilst they are cooking, sauté the spring roll vegetables and set aside to cool.

Pick the meat from the leg bones and add to the vegetables.

Cut one sheet of filo pastry in half; lay one piece on a board, brush with a little melted butter and then lay the second piece on top of the first. Place a small amount of the filling mixture on to the pastry, and fold over to create the spring roll. Bake in the oven at gas mark 4/180°C for 8 minutes or until golden.

For the Rabbit Parfait

You will need four dariole moulds (*see* Glossary), lined with clingfilm.

1 shallot

A shot of brandy

50g/1¾oz rabbit liver

3 eggs

50g/1¾oz butter

2 baby leeks

2 baby carrots

4 baby beetroot

A dash of honey

A little balsamic vinegar

An 'assiette' of rabbit – as created at The Hoste Arms, Norfolk.

Sauté the shallot, add the brandy and cook out the alcohol. Add this to the liver.

Put the eggs, butter and liver into separate containers, and set aside in a warm place in order to bring the temperature of the ingredients up to 37°C. Then add all the ingredients to a food processor and 'blitz' until smooth.

Pass through a fine sieve and pour into the lined dariole moulds; place the moulds in a *bain marie* – or they can be placed in a roasting tin containing water, which will serve the same purpose – to cook at gas mark ¼/110°C for 20 minutes.

Leave to cool and turn out immediately before serving.

Make a mix of vegetables by steaming the two baby leeks and two baby carrots for 2 minutes. Peel and pan fry the baby beetroot in butter, adding a dash of honey and a little balsamic vinegar. Cook until soft.

Assemble the dish as shown in the photograph.

Mustard Rabbit with Butternut Squash and Pumpkin

We all do it – grow pumpkins and squashes in the vegetable garden and then don't know how best to use them once they are matured! There are the obvious things like butternut squash soup (and for the best recipe ever for that see 'Blackfriars Butternut Squash Soup' in our book *The New Country Cook* – also published by The Crowood Press), and the famous American pumpkin pie, recipes that use both in another way entirely.

1 tablespoon olive oil	450g/1lb pumpkin, skinned and cut into cubes
½ tablespoon caraway seeds	½ tablespoon roughly ground pink
3 garlic cloves, peeled and finely sliced	peppercorns (use a pestle and mortar)
1 large rabbit, jointed	1 tablespoon Dijon mustard
115g/4oz butter	150ml/5fl oz cider
450g/1lb butternut squash, skinned	150ml/5fl oz thick cream
and cut into cubes	

On the hob, heat the oil, caraway seeds and garlic in a flameproof casserole dish – don't let the garlic brown and burn. Then add the jointed rabbit and quickly brown each piece in order to seal the meat.

Add the butter and let it melt around the rabbit pieces, then include the squash, pumpkin, peppercorns, mustard and cider. Stir the ingredients as well as you are able, then place the lid on the casserole and cook in the oven at gas mark 4/180°C for about an hour. After this time, check the dish and stir the ingredients again, before cooking for another half hour.

Stir in the cream to the squash/pumpkin rough 'mash' that will have formed during cooking and take immediately to the table.

Wild Rabbit with Wild Sorrel

If you look in any game-oriented recipe book you're almost certain to find at least one variation on this classic French recipe. We didn't want to miss out either, and so are including this one translated from a small pack of recipe cards given away many years ago by the monthly magazine *Le Chasseur Français*.

Sorrel (*Rumex*) can be found growing wild in many parts of France where it is known as *oseille*. It is at its peak in the spring – just in time for when the season's young wild rabbits are maturing to perfection – and is best identified by its elongated spinach-like leaves, which range in colour from dark green through to the colour of young watercress. It is not, however, necessary to go tramping across fields in search of it, as it is occasionally found in greengrocers and at farmers' markets. Also, it is often sold in specialist food shops, already cooked and in tins or jars.

1 wild rabbit, jointed	Salt and pepper
30g/1oz butter	2 egg yolks
Plain flour, as a thickening agent	125ml/4fl oz crème fraîche
500ml/18fl oz vegetable or game stock	350g/12oz wild sorrel, roughly chopped
1 sprig thyme	(reserve a few leaves for garnish)
1 bay leaf	

Prepare the rabbit – as with so many of these recipes – by heating the butter in a frying pan and sealing the rabbit joints on all sides. Add a tablespoon of flour, and stir around the pan with a wooden spoon and cook for a couple of minutes until a smooth paste is formed of the flour, butter and meat juices.

Add the herbs and a little salt and pepper, together with the stock: bring to the boil, stirring all the while, then turn down the heat, cover the pan so that the stock does not evaporate too quickly, and simmer for about three-quarters of an hour.

In a bowl, beat together well the egg yolks and crème fraîche. Set aside until the rabbit is cooked (the meat should come away from the bone when the point of a knife is inserted): remove the rabbit pieces with a slotted spoon, place on a hot plate and cover with foil or similar to keep warm.

Take the bay leaf and thyme from the liquid remaining in the frying pan, and add the sorrel leaves to it. Heat for a minute or so until they begin to wilt. Turn down the heat, spoon in the egg/crème fraîche mix, and stir the sauce gently but continuously until it thickens (this will probably take 3 or 4 minutes).

Finally, return the rabbit to the pan in order for it to warm through and become thoroughly coated with the sauce. Turn out into a serving dish and top with a couple of sorrel leaves as garnish.

Devilled Rabbit

Many years ago, the term 'devilled' was used to describe a variety of odd bits and pieces of game that had been doused in all manner of sauces and were traditionally eaten with the fingers. Nowadays the term is used far more loosely in cooking.

1 rabbit, jointed	Seasoning
Mustard	55g/2oz bacon, chopped

Devilled Rabbit.

1 large onion, thinly sliced	300ml/10fl oz milk, approximately (*see* method below)
1 bay leaf	30g/1oz butter
4 tablespoons water	30g/1oz flour

Soak the rabbit joints in cold salted water overnight. Remove and dry, then coat with mustard and seasoning. Place the joints in a casserole and add the bacon, onion, bay leaf and water. Cover and cook at gas mark 6/200°C for an hour, or until the rabbit is tender.

Strain off the liquid from the casserole, and make up to 300ml/10fl oz with milk.

In a small pan, melt the butter and slowly add the flour in order to make a roux. Gradually add the juice/milk liquid, bring to the boil, and then simmer for 3 minutes, stirring continually.

Place the rabbit joints on a serving plate, cover with the thickened sauce and surround with either boiled long-grain rice or quenelles of mashed potato. For a vegetable, French beans and/or petit pois would go well. Alternatively, try steamed nettles! They taste just like spinach – pick them young, steam and serve with grated nutmeg over the top.

Naan Rabbit Pockets

This lunchtime snack is unusual in that it uses rabbit pieces rather than the chicken or lamb normally associated with such a dish.

3 tablespoons plain, low fat yoghurt
1 very heaped teaspoon garam masala
1 teaspoon salt
3 tablespoons lemon juice
1 tablespoon fresh coriander, finely chopped
1 fresh green chilli, deseeded and finely chopped
450g/1lb rabbit meat, off the bone,
   removed of sinew and diced

1 tablespoon vegetable oil
1 teaspoon chilli powder
4 naan breads
8 thinly sliced onion rings
8 tomato rings
½ white cabbage, finely shredded
Lime, in quarters

In a bowl, mix together the yoghurt, garam masala, salt, lemon juice, fresh coriander, chilli powder and green chilli. Add the diced rabbit, stir well to ensure that all the pieces are coated, and leave to marinate for an hour.

Meanwhile, preheat the grill to very hot and then turn down to medium. Line a grill pan with foil, and once it is sufficiently marinated, spoon in the rabbit mix. Brush with a little of the oil and cook for a total of 15–20 minutes – but be sure in that time to turn the rabbit mixture at least twice, and to apply another coating of oil if necessary.

Cut into the middle of each naan bread to make a 'pocket', and fill each with some of the grilled rabbit mixture, two onion rings, the same of tomato, and a little shredded cabbage. Top with a quarter of a lime (to be squeezed over if desired) and serve immediately – perhaps with an accompanying green salad and extra fresh coriander to accentuate the Indian 'authenticity'.

Pish-Pash Rabbit

'Pish-Pash' is an Indian dish which has always been popular in that particular country – where it is believed that cooking is one of the divine arts, and should be approached as a sacred ceremony. Whilst we wouldn't go that far, there is, we find, a certain reverence and love felt in the preparation (and subsequent enjoyment!) of food shared with friends and family.

1.2ltr/2 pints water
1 tablespoon milk
2 dessertspoons salt
1 rabbit, cut into pieces

225g/8oz long-grained rice
2 medium-sized onions, finely chopped
55g/2oz raisins

In a pan, boil the water, milk and salt: add the rabbit pieces and cook until tender. Remove, and allow to cool sufficiently so you can take the meat from the bone; otherwise, keep warm.

Add the rice and onions to the rabbit stock, and boil for 25 minutes until almost all the stock is absorbed by the rice. Return the rabbit meat to the rice: stir and heat until all the stock has gone – stir frequently so that the rice does not 'catch' the bottom of the pan.

Stir in the raisins, tip into a serving dish, cover with a clean cloth and keep warm until serving. Garnish with fresh coriander if desired.

Marinated Rabbit – Italian Style

There are many rabbit recipes that have an Italian influence, rabbit being a regular ingredient in the traditional rural recipes of that country.

1 rabbit, quartered	1 tablespoon plain flour
55g/2oz lard	8 thick slices of day-old bread
2 thick slices of pancetta, chopped	

For the marinade

2 onions and 2 carrots, peeled and chopped	Small handful each of parsley and
2 glasses of 'heavy' red wine	fresh thyme, roughly chopped
½ glass red wine vinegar	1 bay leaf
½ wine glass olive oil	2 cloves
Salt and pepper	

Chop the rabbit into pieces, discarding its feet and head, and marinate it for at least a day – although to be authentically Italian, two would be better (turn the meat in the marinade several times during that time to ensure that all the meat has been in thorough contact). Remove the rabbit from the marinade and pat dry with kitchen roll; put the marinade aside for later use.

In a heavy-bottomed, flame-proof casserole dish, heat the lard and quickly fry the chopped pancetta. When the fat begins to crackle, add the rabbit quarters and cook, turning them until they are well browned. Remove and keep them warm.

Sift a tablespoon of flour into the pan juices and mix in well, then slowly add and whisk in the marinade. Return the rabbit to the pot. Cover and simmer over a very low flame for 3 hours, stirring often, and adding more water if necessary.

To serve, toast the slices of bread and lay on a serving dish. Spoon the meat over the bread, then the sauce over the meat, and serve immediately.

MARINADES

Marinades help to break down meat fibres as well as imbibing them with subtle tastes. They also counteract the possibility of dryness as the meat cooks. Meat joints should be left in a marinade for at least twelve hours in order to bring out the best flavours. Remember to turn the meat occasionally during that time.

A typical marinade might consist of a bottle of red wine (full bodied rather than the lighter, Gamay grape type), two tablespoons of red wine vinegar (or rather less of balsamic), chopped onion and garlic, herbs, a pinch of mixed dried spices and the same of grated nutmeg, a bay leaf or two, a couple of 'glugs' of olive oil, and if you can get them, half-a-dozen juniper berries. There is, however, a school of thought amongst some professional chefs that the wine only serves to pickle the meat, and in doing so, actually draws out some of the moisture. You may prefer to follow their advice and omit all but the slightest amount of wine, replacing it with rather more olive oil.

A ginger and garlic marinade gives an almost oriental combination, especially if a small amount of soy sauce is added, and is perfect for use with rabbit. Proceed as follows: combine together one finely chopped onion, two crushed cloves of garlic, and a tablespoon of freshly grated ginger plus two teaspoons of chopped parsley. Add liquid consisting of a quarter of a cup of lemon juice, the same of sesame oil, two tablespoons of soy sauce and the same of honey.

Not only will this make an excellent marinade, but the mixture can also be brushed over meat when grilling or barbecuing.

Marinades are used in many rabbit recipes.

Roast Saddle of Rabbit with Braised Leg Faggot and Grain Mustard Spinach Ragout

Simon Cadge is head chef at The Old Bridge Hotel, Huntingdon. He is one of the fortunate ones who can source local produce, and most of his game, rabbits and pigeons come from the nearby Denham estate. He also has a superb traditional butcher not five minutes walk away – no wonder his dishes are so good! Many thanks to Simon, his sous-chef Ben, and to The Old Bridge owner John Hoskins and general manager Nina Beamond for allowing us to use this recipe.

Interestingly, The Old Bridge is associated with the organization known as the Great Inns of Britain, a collection of independent, historic, stylish inns, all renowned for their warm welcome, attentive service and fine food and wine.

1 rabbit	Chopped hard herbs
Duck fat	1 carrot
4 cloves garlic	1 celeriac

To make the ragout

250g/9oz cooked cannelloni beans	Knob of butter
1 teaspoon grain mustard	1 dessertspoonful lemon juice
1 tablespoon cream	250g/9oz baby spinach
2 tablespoons red wine sauce	Salt and pepper
(enough for the faggot and to create a	
paste when added to the ragout)	

Butcher the rabbit by removing all the legs, and gently confit[1] the latter in duck fat together with the garlic for 1–2 hours or until tender.

Remove the bone from the rabbit saddle without damaging any skin; keep all the trim of rabbit, and with it, make a small amount of basic mousse[2] to stuff the saddle.

Once stuffed, roll in clingfilm four or five times and tie both ends, pushing in tight to make a cylinder shape. Poach in boiling water for 10–12 minutes, and refresh[3].

Meanwhile, the rabbit legs should have cooked through sufficiently so you can pick off all the meat, discarding any rubbish. Add a little red wine sauce, squeeze the garlic cloves from their skin, add some chopped hard herbs, and season. Mould into shape and wrap in cropinette[4] then leave to cool. This is the faggot.

Roast the saddle for 8–10 minutes at gas mark 6/200°C, adding the faggot and batons of blanched carrot and celeriac after 4 minutes' cooking.

To make the ragout, put the beans in a pan with the grain mustard, cream, red wine sauce, butter and lemon juice. Reduce gently for 5–10 minutes, and add the baby spinach at the last minute.

Note: Although the following terms are explained in the Glossary, we feel it is prudent to mention them here, too, in order to understand Simon's recipe more fully:

(1) Generally 'confit' is used to describe meat preserved in duck fat, but occasionally it is used as a cooking term to indicate a method whereby fat is heated in a pan, the meat (or sometimes fish such as salmon) is added and submerged until tender, and then used immediately (after being allowed to rest for a short while).

(2) A mousse is a light mixture, either sweet or savoury: the latter often generally contains puréed or blended meats or fish.

(3) The term 'refresh' is usually used by chefs in the sense of either to blanch vegetables in ice-cold water in order to set the colour and restore their crispness, or, in the case of greens and herbs that are still very fresh but have gone limp, to restore them to their original state by placing them in cold water and then patting them dry; occasionally meat and fish are treated in similar fashion to stop them cooking more than is required.

(4) 'Cropinette' is French in origin, but Simon, head chef at The Old Bridge, tells me that 'Cropinette, or caul fat as it is also known in the UK, is the lining of a pig's stomach. It is used to shape and also to protect the food within as it is being roasted.'

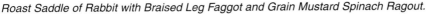

Roast Saddle of Rabbit with Braised Leg Faggot and Grain Mustard Spinach Ragout.

Preparing some of the ingredients for 'Roast Saddle of Rabbit with Braised Leg Faggot'.

Spiced Rabbit and Wholegrain Spaghetti

There are all manner of rabbit dishes that incorporate pasta – in the booklet *Discover the Great Taste of Game* published a few years ago by the Countryside Alliance in conjunction with the National Game Dealer's Association there is a lovely one for 'Rabbit Cacciatore on Tagliatelle'. The following recipe is just about to be incorporated into a similar booklet that promotes the great taste of game, and we are pleased to be able to include it here first!

350g/12oz cooked rabbit meat
225g/8oz wholegrain spaghetti
30g/1oz butter
1 onion, finely chopped
1 garlic clove, finely chopped
1 teaspoon ground coriander
½ teaspoon ground cardamom
2 tablespoons wholegrain flour

150ml/5fl oz plain yoghurt
450ml/15fl oz rabbit or game stock
2 egg yolks
15g/½oz fresh parsley, chopped
115g/4oz wild mushrooms, wiped and quite thinly sliced
50g/1¾oz fresh wholegrain breadcrumbs
30g/1oz Parmesan cheese, grated

Roast or boil a rabbit until the meat can be removed from the bones (save the remainder of the carcass to include in a stockpot) and set aside.

In a pan of boiling water, cook the spaghetti according to the instructions on the packet until it is *al dente*. Drain through a colander, and wash off with boiling water from the kettle.

In a frying pan, sauté the onion in the butter, then add the garlic, coriander and cardamom and cook for about a minute over a medium heat. Sprinkle in the tablespoons of flour, and stir whilst still on the heat. Once the cooking juices have been absorbed by the flour and a *roux* has formed, remove the pan from the hob and gently stir in the yoghurt, and afterwards the stock.

Put back over the heat and stir carefully stir for 3 minutes. Remove once more, and briskly stir in the egg yolks, the chopped parsley, and finally the rabbit pieces.

In a greased, shallow ovenproof dish, spread roughly half of the spaghetti; spoon over and level half of the rabbit mix. Add a layer of the mushrooms, then the remainder of the spaghetti, and then the remaining rabbit mix. In a bowl, mix together the breadcrumbs and grated cheese and spread over as a topping.

Cook at gas mark 4/180°C for three-quarters of an hour. Take to the table immediately.

Congilio Ischitano

Ischia is one of six islands set in the Bay of Naples; the others are Capri and Procida, and the remaining three are uninhabited. It is a major holiday destination for people from Milan, and is approximately half the size of the Isle of Wight. Rabbit, in various guises, is a popular dish with the tourists.

2 tablespoons olive oil	2 sprigs fresh rosemary
2 jointed rabbits or 4 rabbit saddles	300ml/10fl oz red wine
100g/3½oz pancetta or dry-cured	400g/14oz can plum tomatoes
smoked streaky bacon, diced	100ml/3½fl oz fresh chicken stock, hot
3 whole garlic cloves, peeled	1 tablespoon butter, softened
2 red onions	Salt and pepper

Heat the oil in a flameproof casserole or heavy-based saucepan over a medium-high heat. Add the rabbit, in batches, and brown all over. Remove with a slotted spoon and set aside.

Add the bacon to the pan and fry for 2–3 minutes, until well coloured. Add the garlic and brown slightly, then add the onions and cook for 1–2 minutes. Add the rosemary and red wine, allowing the wine to bubble up for a couple of minutes, and then return the rabbit to the pot. Stir well and reduce the heat to a simmer.

Push the tomatoes through a colander into a bowl with the back of a wooden spoon. Add the pulp and the juices to the casserole and fold in well. Add the stock so as to almost cover the meat, cover with a lid and simmer gently for about 1½–2 hours. At the end of this time, check the meat for tenderness, and if necessary, cook a while longer.

Stir the softened butter into the stew and season to taste. Serve with rice, mash or polenta.

Wild Rabbit Saddle in Herb Mousse with Fondant Potato; Leg Ballotine and Wild Mushrooms

We were lucky enough to be directed to The Bell at Horndon on the Hill, Essex, in our search for unusual and interesting rabbit recipes. Better still, the one we found is an award-winning one, a fact of which head chef Stuart Fry is rightly proud. Stuart and Stephen Treadwell could not have been more helpful during our visit, and imparted a great deal of their knowledge on cooking matters with infectious enthusiasm. As can be seen from the photograph that accompanies this recipe, just looking at this particular dish would be enough to make any unsure diners immediately decide that they want to eat rabbit! The Bell is owned by Christine and John Vereker and very ably run by Joanne Butler, their general manager.

2 chicken breasts	Knob of butter
White of one egg	3 cloves garlic
¼ bunch parsley	2 rabbits
¼ bunch tarragon	600ml/1pt chicken stock
¼ bunch chives	Thyme, rosemary
¼ bunch chervil	4 large red potatoes
250g/9oz wild mushrooms	Salt and pepper

To prepare the chicken mousse
Trim off all the fat and sinew from the chicken breasts. Put the meat into a robot coupe and turn on slowly, at the same time adding the egg white and seasoning until it all comes together. Split the mixture into two bowls.

To prepare the herb and mushroom mousses
Chop all the herbs and add to one of the chicken mousses; chill in the fridge for at least 1 hour.
   Sauté the wild mushrooms with a little butter and one clove of garlic without colouring. Allow to cool, and then fold into the second bowl of chicken mousse and chill for at least 1 hour.

To prepare the rabbits
Prepare the rabbits by taking off the back legs and removing the fillets from the saddle. Tunnel-bone the back legs (this involves boning it out around and along the bone without cutting the actual meat so that the stuffing can easily be put in without tying), and trim all excess fat and sinew from the legs and the fillets.
   Spread herb mousse on to clingfilm, place a fillet in the centre, roll up the clingfilm and tie up both ends. Poach in half the chicken stock for 12–15 minutes.
   Fill a piping bag with mushroom mousse mix and fill the tunnel-boned legs; then wrap them in caul fat and place them in a tray with the chicken stock, half the thyme and rosemary, and braise for 1–1½ hours at gas mark 2/150°C.

Wild Rabbit Saddle in Herb Mousse with Fondant Potato – an award-winning dish from The Bell, Horndon on the Hill, Essex.

For the fondant potato
Keeping the oven set at gas mark 2/150°C as for braising the rabbit legs, cut out fondant shapes from the potatoes with a steel ring; top and tail to allow the potato fondant to stand. Melt butter in a frying pan with the other half of the thyme, rosemary and two cloves of garlic. Place the potato in the butter and when coloured, turn over. Pour in chicken stock to half submerge the potato, then put in the oven for approximately 20–30 minutes.

To assemble the dish
To assemble the dish, remove the legs, fillet and potato from the stocks. Pan-fry the legs to give them colour, and slice the bottom off each one so they stand on the plate (see photo). Top and tail the rabbit fillet and stand it next to the legs. Finally place the potato fondant on the plate. Garnish with thyme.

Rabbit in Peanut Sauce

There is a marvellous little recipe book called *The Game and Cheese Book*, written by Alison and Stephen Morrell of Teesdale Game and Poultry, and Malcolm Pearce, a professional writer and author who, amongst other things, is developing 'The Easy Cook' series of recipe books. Many thanks to Stephen, Alison and especially Malcolm, by whose kind permission this copyrighted recipe is reproduced in full.

To feed four people, take one large rabbit, which should be at least a kilo [2¼lb] in weight. Allow for two onions, one clove of garlic and 120 grams [6½oz] unsalted roasted peanuts. You will also need one tablespoon of sweet paprika, half a teaspoon of ground cumin, and salt and pepper for seasoning. Finally, take four tablespoons of olive oil, one tablespoon of white wine vinegar, 150 millilitres [5fl oz] of chicken stock and 300 millilitres [10fl oz] of dry white wine.

Finely grind the roasted peanuts for adding to the dish later on. Heat the olive oil in a casserole and stir in the paprika. Add the rabbit, cut into eight pieces, and then sauté these. Set the rabbit pieces aside and add the finely chopped onions and garlic, cooking these until they are soft. Return all the rabbit pieces to the casserole, mix them well with the vinegar, stock and wine, and cover the dish. Simmer this, turning the rabbit occasionally, until it is tender, which should be in about an hour.

Malcolm further writes:

This is a Chilean recipe, although variations exist elsewhere in Latin America, as with Peru's 'conejo con mani'. Traditionally the latter uses hot peppers as well as the ingredients noted above. The peanuts, which must be unsalted, give the stew a distinctive flavour but they also act as a thickening agent for it. Some variations suggest putting small whole cooked potatoes into the stew just before serving.

Rabbit Goulash

There are many recipes based on Hungarian goulash (Gulyás) – this is just one of them, and it actually originates from Austria!

115g/4oz bacon, chopped	1 tablespoon paprika
1 large onion, chopped	Salt and pepper
30g/1oz beef dripping	2 garlic cloves, peeled and crushed
1kg/2¼lb rabbit meat, boned	600ml/1 pint red wine or cider
and cut into cubes	150ml/5fl oz chicken or game stock
55g/2oz plain flour	150ml/5fl oz sour cream

Fry the bacon and onions gently in the dripping for 10 minutes. Brown the rabbit meat on all sides, then gently sauté the meat, bacon and onions for a further 10 minutes.

Sprinkle in the flour and paprika; add the salt and pepper, and the garlic. Stir and blend thoroughly. Add the wine and enough stock to well cover the meat, and cook in a low oven at gas mark 3/170°C for 2 hours or until tender.

Five minutes before serving, stir in the sour cream and reheat (without boiling). Serve with rice, or to be truly authentic, nockerl (see page 79).

Pan-Fried Rabbit Fillet with Slow Casserole of Leg Meat.

Pan-Fried Rabbit Fillet with Slow Casserole of Leg Meat

This recipe is from Chris and Alison Davy at the Rose and Crown, Romaldkirk, Barnard Castle, Co. Durham. The Rose and Crown (referred to by its many patrons and guests as the 'R & C', in the same way that the Victoria and Albert Museum in London is known as the 'V & A') is a delightfully restful place situated next to the church on the picturesque village green. As well as a cosy lounge and a very welcoming bar, it has a formal restaurant and a busy bistro, which, when we visited, was full of locals – always a sign of good food and friendly staff! Set in real shooting country, the 'R & C' is a regular stop-over for grouse-shooting guests. If you ever visit, look out for the many cookery awards won by Chris, which, quite rightly, are in full view as you walk towards the reception desk.

For the marinade

Cold water (enough to cover the rabbit fillets)   3–4 juniper berries
1 tablespoon olive oil   1 bay leaf

For the casserole

1 rabbit	30g/1oz plain flour
1 onion, sliced	150ml/5fl oz cider
1 carrot, diced small	2 tablespoons Calvados
1 tablespoon tomato purée	55g/2oz chilled, unsalted butter
600ml/1 pint red wine	Seasoning

Marinade the two rabbit fillets in a little oil, water, bay leaf and juniper. Seal the two legs in a little butter and oil. Remove and put in a casserole. Sauté the onion and carrot for 5 minutes. Add the tomato purée, flour and red wine, cover and cook in the oven at gas mark 4/180°C for 1 hour until tender. Season to taste.

Sauté the rabbit fillets for 5 minutes or until cooked. Remove from the pan and keep warm. Deglaze the pan with the cider, and reduce to half. Add the Calvados and reduce again, then whisk in the chilled butter. Season.

Serve a casseroled leg with the cooking juices spooned over; slice the fillet in two, and pour the Calvados sauce over.

Note: Chris says that butter is added to the sauce in order to create a 'shine' to the finish – the butter must, however, be chilled.

Stuffed, Apricot-Glazed Leg of Rabbit

As in a couple of the other recipes we feature in these pages, you will need to tunnel-bone the rabbit legs. Once you've done one, you'll find it quite easy, but if possible, ask a butcher or someone experienced to show you how to do this for the first time. Basically, it is just a question of cutting round the leg bone from the haunch end with a thin, long-bladed knife. Do the boning on a wooden board – not whilst holding the leg in your hand, which would be a recipe for disaster rather than an interesting rabbit dish!

Serves eight

8 rabbit back legs, tunnel-boned and opened out to make a 'pocket'	150ml/5fl oz rabbit, chicken or vegetable stock
30g/1oz butter	150g/5½oz breakfast branflakes, slightly crushed but not pulverized
55g/2oz mushrooms, sliced	1 x 175g/6oz tin water-chestnuts, chopped
1 large onion, finely chopped	Salt and pepper
1 stick celery, split lengthways down the middle and finely chopped	Pinch dried sage

For the sauce

350g/12oz apricot jam or conserve	1 tablespoon tomato ketchup
2 tablespoons mayonnaise	½ teaspoon English mustard powder

Make the sauce by combining the jam, mayonnaise, tomato ketchup and mustard powder together in a mixing bowl. Set aside.

In a frying pan, use the butter to sauté the mushrooms, onion and celery; cook until tender.

In another bowl combine the stock and the breakfast branflakes, and leave to stand until all the stock is absorbed. Add the chestnuts, and the vegetables from the frying pan. Season with the salt, pepper and sage.

Use a little of the mix to stuff each of the rabbit legs in the hole where the bone has been removed. Place them in a greased, shallow ovenproof dish and spoon over the apricot sauce mixture. Bake at gas mark 4/180°C for three-quarters of an hour, or until the rabbit legs are tender.

Wild Rabbit Soup

We included 'Hungarian Pigeon Soup' in *The Pigeon Cook* (also published by The Crowood Press), and so thought it only fair to provide something similar here that uses rabbit. Traditionally, the idea behind most soups is that they make a nourishing meal from leftover meats, fish and vegetables: indeed there are recipes that suggest incorporating even the skinned head of a rabbit into a broth – personally we think that might be just a step too far, but this recipe is certainly one way of utilizing the front legs, neck and ribcage whilst retaining the far more fleshy back legs and saddle parts for another purpose.

The front half of a wild rabbit, jointed and chopped through the bones

55g/2oz butter	Salt and pepper for seasoning
1 onion, peeled and roughly sliced	2ltr/3½ pints beef stock
55g/2oz bacon, roughly chopped	45g/1½oz flour
1 stick celery, roughly sliced	Small wineglass of port
1 carrot, scraped and chopped	1 teaspoon redcurrant jelly
½ small turnip, peeled and diced	Lemon juice
Bouquet garni	

In a large heavy-bottomed pan, fry the meat pieces in the butter together with the onion and bacon pieces for about 5 minutes or until well browned (take care not to let the butter burn, or this will taint the soup). Add the remaining vegetables, the bouquet garni, salt and pepper and beef stock. Cover and simmer for 3 to 4 hours.

When the meat is soft and falling off the bones, strain off the liquid through a sieve, and with the back of a wooden spoon, push as much as is possible of the rabbit meat and vegetables through. Put to one side and allow to go cold – after which time a fatty layer may have formed on the surface. Skim before re-heating the liquid.

Blend the flour and port together and make a paste; add a little of the hot soup, mix and then return all to the pan whilst at the same time adding the teaspoon of redcurrant jelly. Bring to the boil, stirring continuously until the soup begins to thicken nicely; then cook for another 5 minutes before finally including a squeeze of lemon juice.

Serve immediately.

A slow cooker is perfect for making all manner of rabbit soups, stews and casseroles.

Rabbit Stew with Olives

Slow cooking is the name of the game when it comes to producing perfect stews. A slow cooker might be worth the investment if you intend doing a great deal of this sort of recipe, but for the occasional dish, a traditional hob/oven-proof casserole will serve the purpose well.

3 tablespoons olive oil
4 cloves garlic, peeled and minced
1 tablespoon fresh rosemary, finely chopped
1 rabbit, jointed and seasoned
115g/4fl oz red wine
1 tablespoon tomato purée

250ml/8fl oz chicken or rabbit stock
1 tablespoon chopped parsley leaves
55–115g/2–4oz black olives, stoned and
    split or pricked with a fork
Sea salt and freshly ground black pepper

Heat the olive oil in a large oven-proof casserole with a lid. Add the garlic and rosemary, and cook briefly, taking care not to burn the garlic. Add the rabbit pieces, browning them evenly. Add the wine gradually, followed by the tomato purée, stock, parsley, olives and seasoning.

Cover the pan and cook over a low heat or in a slow oven until the rabbit is tender – about 45–60 minutes. If the sauce is too thin, remove the meat with a slotted spoon to a warm plate, and increase the heat in order to reduce the liquid.

South American Rabbit Stew (Cazuela)

Never wanting to miss an opportunity, when we discovered that the son of a friend of ours was working on an Argentinean cattle ranch, we contacted him straightaway to see if he could find us a typical local dish that used rabbit as one of its ingredients. He promised to ask the cook who looked after all the farm hands at lunchtime, and as good as his word, eventually sent us the following recipe, written exactly as the cook had described the dish to him. Therefore our very grateful thanks to Richard Campbell for all his help.

Note: The slow cooking time involved would, we imagine, make it a good recipe for older rabbits.

2 rabbits, jointed
Plain flour for dusting
Olive oil, for frying
Herb sachet (suitable herbs tied in a small piece of muslin)
8 medium-sized potatoes, peeled but whole
1 small pumpkin, peeled, deseeded and cut into 7.5cm/3in cubes
225g/8oz French/runner beans, topped and tailed and sliced

225g/8oz peas/broad beans
115g/4oz uncooked rice
2 ears of sweetcorn, cooked (there's no reason why you shouldn't used tinned sweetcorn, but we thought you'd better have the recipe as it was given to us!)
Salt and pepper
1 egg

Flour the rabbit joints, and in a heavy-bottomed hob-proof casserole, sauté in oil to seal. Carefully (you don't want the oil to 'spit' as you do so) add just enough cold water to cover. Add the sachet of herbs: bring to the boil, then turn the heat down to simmer (the liquid should never be allowed to boil again).

Cover and cook for an hour, occasionally skimming off any fat residue forming on the top of the liquid. After the hour is up, remove the sachet of herbs. Add the potatoes, and cook for a further 20 minutes; then add the pumpkin, peas and beans.

Cook for 15 minutes; then add the rice, and continue to cook for another 10 minutes or so. Finally add the sweetcorn, salt and pepper, and cook for 5 minutes more.

Remove the dish from the hob and allow to cool slightly; then break in the raw egg and stir briskly until the liquid has thickened and looks smooth.

Serve the 'cazuela' in bowls, and although you might need a knife and fork to get the last bits or the rabbit meat from the bones, you could always try eating with a spoon and pulling off the meat with fingers and teeth in true gaucho style!

Peppers Stuffed with Rabbit

A traditional Italian country recipe, which would make an interesting starter at any dinner party, or could be eaten as a light lunch accompanied by salad. The fact that the peppers are stuffed with rabbit, rather than the rabbit stuffed with peppers, makes it a little different!

4 peppers	1 glass dry white wine
1 rabbit, the flesh cut from the bones	1 wineglass chicken stock
1 tablespoon softened butter	Tomato paste
1 double handful sliced mushrooms	

Cut the tops off the peppers and keep. Scrape out the insides. Bake at gas mark 4/350°C for 20 minutes, no more.

Meanwhile, fry the rabbit, cut into small pieces, in some butter. Add the sliced mushrooms and the glass of white wine; allow to evaporate slowly. Add the chicken stock and a little tomato paste.

Cook gently for another 10 minutes, then spoon into the peppers. Replace the lids and bake for 15 minutes.

James Rogers' Rabbit Pie

James Rogers and his brother Charles co-own The Dog at Grundisburgh, Suffolk, and they are an award-winning combination: James has won many Food Excellence certificates, and Charles, who works 'front of house', has been awarded the highly regarded Cask Marque accreditation for serving the perfect pint of cask-conditioned ale. Says James:

> Dishes such as rabbit pie are quick and easy and offer superb value. You can get up to around 1½lb – 700 grams – of meat from a rabbit, and here's my recipe for making a rabbit pie that will serve up to ten generous portions, making for seconds and dinners to be enjoyed later in the week.

To make the short-crust pastry

500g/1½lb plain flour	Pinch of mixed herbs
250g/9oz salted butter	Water to bind

Rub the flour and butter together until you achieve a breadcrumb consistency; add a pinch of mixed herbs and six to eight tablespoons of water to bind, and mix all together into a ball. Chill for 20 minutes, then roll out to line a pie dish (James uses a 28cm/11in loose-bottomed flan tin about 2.25cm/1–1¼in deep).

For the pie filling

Vegetable oil for frying	Thyme, bay and rosemary
Meat of three fresh rabbits	3 tablespoons flour
Gammon trim or 150g/5½oz catering bacon	Glass of white wine or light beer or cider
55g/2oz salted butter	300ml/10fl oz chicken stock
1 large Spanish onion, diced	300ml/10fl oz vegetable stock
4 cloves crushed garlic	Zest of a lemon
2 carrots, diced	Egg wash
2 sticks celery, diced	

While the pastry is chilling, seal the rabbit meat in a hot pan with the bacon, and reserve.

Gently soften the onion, garlic, carrots and celery in the butter in a heavy-based pan with the herbs, then add the sealed rabbit and any juices along with the flour, and stir until coated.

Add the wine, and bring up the heat; add the stock and lemon zest, and allow to simmer slowly for approximately 1 hour or until the rabbit is tender, but still holds its shape.

Now roll out the pastry to approximately 3mm/⅛in thick, and line your dish. Add the rabbit using a slotted spoon, and add the sauce/juices at the end to taste (James likes to cook the rabbit without too much liquid, and makes super gravy out of the remaining liquor). Top off with pastry, brush with an egg wash, and bake for 30 minutes in a moderate oven until golden.

James Rogers likes to serve his pie with 'bubble and squeak' (see Chapter 3 page 73), which, he says, is 'just fantastic'. He further comments that:

> If I were cooking this dish for myself I would add all the rabbit offal to the dish, but this is not to everybody's taste. The kidneys are great devilled and served on toast for breakfast, and the livers are great pan-fried with a little port or sherry. The addition of swede, turnip, leek, potato or forcemeat balls will extend the dish even further, and will certainly not compromise either quality or taste.

As well as rabbit pie, James Rogers at The Dog, Grundisburgh, is also known for his Morroccan-style rabbit tagine . . .

and a rabbit terrine much favoured by his regulars.

Brother Charles adds: 'What better to wash it down with than a real East Anglian ale – perhaps try something from Greene King or Adnams.'

Rabbit and Bacon Pudding

The traditional way of cooking young wild rabbit is to do no more than fry the joints along with a rasher or two of bacon. The following recipe takes the idea a bit further, and turns it into a filling winter dish to be enjoyed after a day in the countryside. Have it with a pint of local beer, and afterwards doze by a roaring log fire!

Note: Although once it is prepared you can leave this dish to its own devices, you will nevertheless need to keep a careful eye on the water level in the steaming pan.

2 young rabbits, jointed – cut the legs in half and the back into 3–4 pieces
Seasoned flour

175g/6oz thick bacon rashers
1 rounded tablespoon of finely chopped chives
125ml/4fl oz vegetable or chicken stock

For the suet crust
225g/8oz self-raising flour
100g/3½oz fresh breadcrumbs
150g/5½oz shredded suet

Salt and pepper
150ml/5fl oz cold water

Soak the jointed and trimmed rabbits overnight in salted water; then rinse and dry thoroughly, and roll in the seasoned flour. Cut the bacon into cubes.

Grease an 850ml/1½ pint pudding bowl.

To prepare the suet crust: mix together all the dry ingredients, then add the water to make a soft dough. Roll out two-thirds of the dough, and line the greased pudding basin with it.

Pack the rabbit pieces and bacon into the basin, add the chives, and pour in the stock. Roll out the remaining pastry and make a lid to cover the top of the pudding; press down well at the edges. Cover tightly with foil, and steam for 3 hours.

For a bit of rural authenticity, serve the pudding to the table wrapped round with a clean gingham tea towel!

Lawrence and Julia Murphy's Rabbit Pie; Roasted Loins and Cider Velouté

James Rogers suggests that instead of adding white wine to his rabbit pie you could use light ale or cider. Lawrence and Julia Murphy who own Fat Olives ('Friendly Food – Tasty People'!) at Emsworth, Hampshire, also use a glass of cider in their recipe for rabbit pie and velouté. According to Philip who has tried it, 'It's absolutely marvellous!' The quantities given will make two pies.

For the braising mixture

1 wild rabbit, jointed and the loins removed

1 onion, peeled and roughly chopped

1 large stick celery, chopped

1 leek, chopped

1 carrot, scraped and chopped

500ml/1pt chicken stock (approximately)

1 bay leaf

3–4 peppercorns

Put the legs, together with an onion, celery, leek, carrot and chicken stock, plus a bay leaf and peppercorns, in a casserole dish and braise for 2½ hours in the oven at gas mark 3/150°C. Check that the meat is tender, and allow to cool. Strain the stock, take the meat from the bones and reserve.

For the pie crust

225g/8oz plain flour

150g/5½oz butter

Pinch of salt

1 egg

Tablespoon cold water

Rub the flour and butter together until the mix has the consistency of breadcrumbs. Add the salt, egg and water to make a dough. Cover with clingfilm, and leave in the fridge to chill.

For the pie filling

1 onion, diced

A little butter

30g/1oz flour

1 glass of cider

½ pint rabbit stock (taken from the braise – see above)

125ml/4fl oz double cream

1 leek, thickly sliced

Gently cook the diced onion in butter. Add the flour and cook for a minute. Add the cider, stirring constantly, then add the stock and cream until you have a thick consistency. Add the leek and a little stock from the meat. Allow to cool, then include the rabbit meat.

Roll out the pastry and line the pie tins. Fill with the rabbit mix; cover with pastry, crimp the edges and glaze with egg wash. Place in the fridge until ready to cook.

For the velouté

1 onion, chopped

½ leek, chopped

Butter

1 glass of cider

150ml/5fl oz rabbit stock

150ml/5fl oz cream

Sweat the onion and leek in butter, add the cider and reduce by half; add the stock and further reduce. Pour in the cream and gently cook out, keeping the finished sauce light in texture. Correct the seasoning if required.

Assemble all by placing the pies into a hot oven at gas mark 8/230°C for 15–18 minutes. Pan-fry the loins in a little butter and oil, place in the oven for 3 minutes, then remove and rest.

Lawrence and Julia Murphy's Cider Rabbit Pie.

Meanwhile, warm the velouté and bring it to a froth with a stick blender. Place the pie on the plate, slice the loin, and decorate with juliennes of apple and pea shoots. Spoon the frothy sauce over the loin, and serve immediately.

Dorset Rabbit

A traditional recipe from the days when the farmer's wife would be expected to feed the family and yet help out around the farm – she therefore needed a dish she could prepare and put in the oven at a low heat and go away and leave for a couple of hours.

2 small young rabbits, jointed
Seasoned flour
175g/6oz streaky bacon rashers

For the crust
4 onions
55g/2oz butter
225g/8oz fresh breadcrumbs
Grated zest of half a lemon

Salt and pepper
2 tablespoons finely chopped fresh sage
125ml/4fl oz milk

3 tablespoons chopped parsley
1 egg
A little milk to bind, if necessary

Soak the rabbit joints overnight in plenty of cold, salted water. The next day rinse and dry them, then roll them in the seasoned flour and place in a deep ovenproof dish. Pour on the milk, season the joints well, and sprinkle the sage over.

Cut any rind from the bacon and cut into strips, and scatter over the top of the rabbit pieces.

To make the crust: chop the onions finely, cook in the butter until they turn golden brown, then place into a mixing bowl. Let the onions cool, and then add the crumbs, lemon zest and chopped parsley. Bind with the egg, adding a little milk if necessary, but being careful not to get the mixture wet. Spread over the rabbit and cook at gas mark 3/170°C for approximately 2 hours or until the rabbit is tender and the top browned. If the top looks as if it might be cooked before the meat is, cover it with baking parchment to prevent over-browning.

The Rising Sun Rabbit Pie

Continuing with the rabbit pie theme (*see also* 'James Rogers' Rabbit Pie' and 'Lawrence and Julia Murphy's Rabbit Pie; Roasted Loins and Cider Velouté'), The Rising Sun is a lovely little pub set in the Milland valley halfway between Liphook and Petersfield in Hampshire. Ben Burston is 'mine host', and Richard Bridgens his head chef. As well as their excellent rabbit pie, which features here, they make an equally delightful rabbit terrine, the recipe for which is on page 27.

For the filling

1 rabbit, skinned and jointed	600ml/1 pint water
2 medium onions	Nutmeg, grated
1 medium to large cooking apple, chopped	2 tablespoons Dijon mustard
225g/8oz pancetta, diced	30ml/1fl oz double cream
1 bay leaf	Seasoning
300ml/10fl oz dry cider	

Place all the ingredients (except the mustard and cream) into a saucepan, and bring to the boil; then reduce the heat and simmer for an hour, or until the rabbit is tender. Skim off any fat residue, and remove from the heat. Sieve, saving the stock. Place the pan of stock back on the hob, and reduce by nearly a third.

Meanwhile, pull out the joints of rabbit and strip the meat from the bone in large chunks. Throw the bones away, but save the pieces of vegetable from the broth.

Make up a small roux (approximately 40g/1¼oz fat and 40g/1¼oz flour), make into a smooth paste and stir in the mustard and the cream. Put on the hob and cook out the floury taste ('You can chop parsley into the roux at this point,' says Richard); then add this to the pan of reduced stock and bring back to the simmer.

Take off the hob, and stir in the sieved ingredients and rabbit meat from earlier. Pour this mix into a 1.5ltr/3 pint pie dish, and top with suet pastry.

The Rising Sun Rabbit Pie.

For the suet pastry

350g/12oz self-raising flour

175g/6oz shredded suet, seasoning

Cold water to mix

(Do not over-mix, and use immediately!)

Roll out the suet pastry and lay it over the filled pie dish; fold over and pinch the edges to form a seal, poke a few steam holes in the middle of the pastry, and brush with milk. Place the pie into a pre-heated oven at gas mark 6/220°C for 30 minutes, or until golden brown.

Lapin en Cidre

Living in France, Jeremy notices that almost every rural home still has its pen of rabbits outside the back door, that the weekend sportsmen around his home are never happier than when they've 'bagged' a rabbit, and that the meat sections of all the supermarkets always contain a good supply of rabbit meat. No wonder, then, that the French have so many traditional rabbit recipes, of which this is but one. Note 'Lawrence and Julia Murphy's Rabbit Pie; Roasted Loins and Cider Velouté', which also combines rabbit and cider: it is open to speculation whether the latter has its origins in France or in the West Country, where both the main ingredient and its liquid accompaniment can be found in abundance. Either way, both recipes use them to their best possible advantage.

Olive oil

2 rabbits, jointed

450g/1lb shallots

3 sprigs thyme

2 bay leaves	1 ltr/1¾ pints cider
2 juniper berries	225g/8oz breadcrumbs
1 teaspoon coriander seeds	1 teaspoon saffron

Heat a good 'glug' of olive oil in the bottom of a casserole dish, and fry off the rabbit joints until they are sealed on all sides. Add the shallots, herbs and spices, and cover with cider.

Place the lid on the casserole, and cook in the oven at gas mark 6/200°C for about an hour; at this point check that the meat is still covered by liquid (top up with more cider if necessary), and then lower the oven temperature to gas mark 4/180°C for another hour.

Once cooked, transfer the cooked rabbit joints to a warming plate and strain the casserole juices into a saucepan; then add the breadcrumbs and saffron, and bring the temperature up to the boil. Serve the resultant sauce poured over the rabbit pieces. Accompany with either boiled, or minted and buttered new potatoes.

Note that traditionally the French do not serve their main course with any vegetables other than potatoes.

Rabbit with Prunes and Mustard

700g/1lb 8oz rabbit pieces	175g/6oz ready-to-eat dried prunes
1 tablespoon plain flour	115g/4oz fromage frais
1 tablespoon each of vegetable oil	1 tablespoon Dijon mustard
and softened butter	Seasoning, to taste
1 onion, finely chopped	

Place the rabbit pieces into a polythene bag together with the flour, and shake to coat evenly. Heat the oil and butter in a large pan, and fry the rabbit until golden brown all over.

Add the onions and prunes to the pan, and pour over just enough water to cover. Season generously and simmer for 45 minutes, or until the rabbit is tender.

Remove the rabbit with a slotted spoon and keep warm. Stir the fromage frais and mustard into the pan, and simmer until reduced slightly. Spoon the sauce over the rabbit, and serve with mashed potatoes and broccoli or green beans.

Rabbit with Prunes and Raisins

Several rabbit recipes incorporate a sweet/sour element; others suggest including prunes – a popular addition to many rabbit dishes. In this recipe, one gets the best of both worlds! It comes from a hand-written recipe found in an extremely tatty copy of *The Belling Guide to Cooking with Electric* – presumably given away in the 1940s/1950s to purchasers of new ovens.

1kg/2¼lb rabbit meat	1 bay leaf
300ml/10fl oz dry white wine	2 tablespoons redcurrant jelly
175g/6oz onions, peeled and sliced	A few peppercorns
300ml/10fl oz chicken stock	8 whole prunes, stoned

55g/2oz seedless raisins
1 tablespoon malt vinegar
2 teaspoons cornflour

Sea salt and freshly ground black pepper
(as seasoning)
Chopped fresh parsley and dry fried
almonds (for garnish)

Marinade the rabbit meat overnight in the wine and onions. Next day discard the onions, and put the rabbit and wine into a hobproof casserole dish. Pour in the chicken stock; add the bay leaf, redcurrant jelly and the peppercorns. Bring to the boil.

Add the prunes and raisins; place the lid on the dish and cook at gas mark 3/170°C for about 1½ hours, or until the rabbit is tender and the prunes look swollen.

Allow to cool, then remove the meat from the bones. Strain the liquor into a clean pan (retaining the prunes and raisins). Add the vinegar blended with the cornflour, and boil for a couple of minutes.

Place the rabbit meat, prunes and raisins in a warmed serving dish, then pour the sauce over. Garnish with the chopped fresh parsley and almonds.

Vendée Rabbit with Shallots and Mushrooms

The Vendée department of western France can be a bleak place in the winter, but the wild rabbits seem to like it! Those nearer the coast graze on vegetation that has been covered by the salty sea water during particularly rough times, and the farmers there claim that it imparts a delicate subtle salty taste to the rabbit's flesh when cooked. Be that as it may, this is a recipe from the area.

2 small tender rabbits, jointed
1 sprig thyme
100g/3½oz bacon lardons
225g/8oz field mushrooms,
    thickly sliced

100g/3½oz butter (the French sort containing
    granules of sea salt, if you can get it)
Freshly ground black pepper

For the marinade
500ml/18fl oz white wine
1 carrot, scraped and sliced

3 decent sized shallots, peeled and finely chopped
1 sprig thyme

In a bowl, mix together the marinade ingredients, add the rabbit pieces, cover and leave overnight. The next day, remove the rabbits, but keep hold of the marinade and its contents because it will be used again to cook the rabbit joints.

Cook the bacon lardons in the bottom of a large heavy pan until they have lost all their fat. Seal the rabbit joints in the bacon fat, and with a slotted spoon remove the joints and the bacon pieces. Place to one side, and gently fry the shallots from the marinade, and the mushrooms. Remove with the spoon and also place to one side.

Using a sieve, strain the marinade liquid into the pan; boil, and as soon as it has, turn down the heat until it is just simmering. Replace the rabbit and bacon pieces and roughly half of the mushroom/shallot mix, together with the other sprig of herb. Place the lid on the pan and cook gently for about an hour, during which time, check and occasionally stir the ingredients with a wooden spoon. At the finish of cooking, remove the rabbit pieces with the slotted spoon and place in a warming cover or on a warmed plate covered by thick foil.

Turn up the heat under the pan and allow the liquid to reduce by around half. Take the pan from the hob, and turn down the heat. Dice the butter and gradually stir into the sauce (this has the effect of giving it an attractive 'glaze').

For the final time, add the rabbit joints to the pan, together with the remaining shallot/mushroom mix, and heat through before serving.

Potato and Rabbit Lemon-Flavoured Dauphinoise

There cannot be many recipes easier than this one – potatoes and meat done at once, and not much washing-up to do, either – what more could one ask for? Serve with any of the green vegetables suggested in the next chapter 'Trimmings and Accompaniments'.

1 rabbit, jointed and cut into portions	200ml/7fl oz cold water
1kg/2¼lb potatoes, peeled and thickly sliced or cubed	Juice of 2 lemons
	Salt and pepper
200ml/7fl oz olive oil	Pinch of oregano

Place the rabbit pieces in an ovenproof dish or casserole and add the potatoes, oil, water, lemon juice and seasoning. Cover and cook for 1 hour at gas mark 6/200°C.

Greek Traditional Rabbit Stew (Stifado)

You will find this traditional Greek dish mentioned in many books that contain rabbit recipes. Philip picked up this one whilst on holiday at the Medusa Resort Hotel, Naxos, Greece. It was given to him by Mariangela Karlovitch.

Note: This recipe has not been tried by the authors and was translated from Greek into English by Mariangela and appears exactly as set out by her. Looking at it, there is no reason in the world why the basic ingredients and method should not be adapted in order to create a conventional casserole.

1 rabbit, cut into pieces	1 cinnamon stick
1 large onion, finely chopped	2 cloves garlic cut in pieces
1kg/2¼lb baby onions	Ground black pepper
850ml/1½ pints olive oil	1 stock cube concentrated vegetables
1 small glass vodka or Metaxa brandy	and herbs, diluted in half a cup
4 ripened tomatoes, peeled and finely chopped	of hot water (instead of salt)
½ carton or tin of concentrated tomato juice	1 dessertspoon softened butter
2 bay leaves	1 cup water

Stifado, as served at The Medusa Resort Hotel, Naxos, Greece.

Wash the rabbit pieces. Fry the onions in the butter until brown (but not burnt). Place the rabbit, onion and oil into a pressure cooker. Pour in the vodka or brandy and add the rest of the ingredients. Cook for half an hour on a very low heat.

RILLETTES MÉNAGÈRES

The simple *rillettes* or *pâtés ménagères* of France are all highly individual as the recipes vary not only in different regions, but often from one village to another. This particular recipe has its origins in the Loire Valley area around the town of Tours.

Take two rabbits, bone them, and dice the meat.

Dice 2kg/4½lb lean pork tenderloin, and 1.25kg/2lb 12oz fat pork.

Pour 1ltr/1¾ pints of water into a large heavy-bottomed pan, together with half a teaspoon of salt per 450g/1lb of meat being cooked.

Then add first the fat pork, then the lean, and finally the rabbit.

Let it cook over a moderate heat for 2½ hours, taking care not to let the meat 'catch' the pan bottom. Alternatively, cook in a casserole dish in a moderate oven, gas mark 4/180°C, for the same length of time.

When it is almost cooked, and the meat can be crushed with a fork, mash it lightly. When it begins to brown, remove from the heat and pour in a glass of white wine.

Cover the pot with a cloth and let it stand for a few minutes before packing the *rillettes* into sealed and sterilized storage jars (in France they are traditionally earthenware). Because of the fat pork content, they should keep for quite a time – some makers claiming several months.

Barbecued Rabbit with Saffron and Yoghurt

Because it is necessary to cut the uncooked rabbit into chunks suitable for skewering and barbecuing, this particular recipe can be quite wasteful of rabbit (although the remainder of the carcass can be used to make excellent stock). One rabbit cooked in such a way will suffice for two people – for bigger numbers, use more rabbits and increase the quantities of the other ingredients accordingly.

1 young rabbit, cut as best as possible into
    pieces suitable for barbecuing
Plain yoghurt (enough to pour over and
    cover the rabbit)

1 medium-sized onion, finely chopped
3 tablespoons of lemon juice
A dash of soy sauce
¼ teaspoon saffron

In a bowl large enough to hold them, marinade the rabbit pieces in the yoghurt, onion, lemon juice, soy sauce and saffron (as saffron doesn't mix evenly with the yogurt, the best way is to soak it in half an egg-cup of very hot water for 10–15 minutes before adding it to the marinade, water and all). Cover and leave in the fridge overnight.

Remove the rabbit chunks from the marinade, skewer, brush the rabbit pieces with olive oil or melted butter and cook over a very hot barbecue. Cook until it is very slightly blackened round the edges and cooked through to the middle.

Serve with Basmati rice and skewered vegetables such as courgette and button mushrooms brushed with the remainder of the yoghurt marinade and also cooked over the barbecue.

Philip's Paella Valenciana with Rabbit

This is one of Philip's 'signature' dishes, which he adapted many years ago from a typical Spanish recipe. There are many variations of this dish and you may add as many (or as little) of the seafood ingredients such as prawns or mussels as you wish. In its true form, paella was originally a peasant dish from the rice fields around Valencia, and local rabbit provided a cheap and plentiful source of protein for this spectacular recipe. Traditionally, paella should be enjoyed over an extensive lunch before the afternoon siesta – and not in the evening!

2 tablespoons olive oil
1 onion, peeled and finely chopped
2 garlic cloves, finely chopped

100ml/3½fl oz tomato purée
2 bay leaves
175g/6oz rabbit, chopped across the bone into
    2cm/¾in pieces

450g/1lb Calasparra or other good paella rice
Pinch paprika
Pinch saffron
1.2ltr/2 pints game or fish stock
1 large glass dry white wine
A double handful *haricots verts*, chopped to 2cm
    (¾in) slices
Salt and freshly ground black pepper

450g/1lb pack seafood selection
Single handful frozen peas
Boil-in-the-bag mussels, or fresh if possible
30g/1oz parsley flakes or fresh chopped
    parsley
1 lemon, quartered
4–6 medium-sized cooked prawns for
    decoration

Heat the oil in a *paellera* (paella pan) or large frying pan over a low heat, then add the onion and cook until softened and transparent; this will take approximately 5–8 minutes. (Avoid browning either the onion or the rice.) Prepare the mussels, then add the garlic, tomato purée, bay leaves and rabbit, and cook for a further 5–7 minutes or until the rabbit is cooked through.

Add the rice, paprika and saffron, and mix to combine. Fry for 2 or 3 minutes, then gradually add the stock, wine and *haricots verts*: bring to the boil and continue to cook for 2–3 minutes, then reduce the heat to a gentle simmer and cook for a further 18 minutes, stirring occasionally during the beginning of the cooking. Watch the paella does not boil dry, although it should be fairly dry at the end of the cooking time with perhaps a little moisture left in the bottom of the pan. Season to taste with a little salt and freshly ground black pepper.

Add the cooked seafood selection and frozen peas; push gently down into the rice and continue to cook 2–3 minutes. Do not stir too much as this will fracture the rice.

Paella Valenciana with Rabbit.

Add the mussels now, either boiled in the bag or cooked separately. Fork them in very lightly.

Remove the pan from the heat, cover with foil – or more traditionally newspaper – and leave to stand for 5 minutes: this is vital for good, fluffy rice. Finish with more parsley and lemon wedges to decorate. Add the cooked prawns round the edge, then serve immediately.

Quick Rabbit Liver Pâté

This just has to be one of the quickest ways ever to create a delicious pâté and is a good way of using up the rabbit livers that you've had in the freezer but were unsure how to use them! It has been adapted from an old recipe found in a cook book of the late 1890s.

30g/1oz butter	225g/8oz rabbit livers, cleaned and chopped
1 small onion, finely chopped	1 teaspoon dried thyme
1 clove garlic, crushed together with a	2 tablespoons brandy
teaspoon of sea salt	Salt and freshly ground black pepper for seasoning

Melt half the butter in a frying pan and gently fry the onion, garlic, livers and thyme for between 5 and 10 minutes, or until the juices of the rabbit livers are only slightly pink. Remove from the heat and leave to cool.

Mince the mixture finely, or use a blender until it is smooth. In a bowl, work in the remaining butter and brandy using a small wooden spoon, then season to taste. Press down firmly, and refrigerate.

Serve on toast as a starter or appetizer.

Rabbit Liver and Rocket Bruschetta

To make the bruschetta (pronounced 'brusketta'), take four slices of French loaf cut on the diagonal, and in a very hot ridged griddle pan, cook on both sides until golden brown. Alternatively use a conventional grill, or during the summer months, a barbecue. Make three cuts into each slice of toasted bread and rub in garlic, then finally drizzle over with good quality olive oil.

3 tablespoons olive oil	225g/8oz rabbit livers
1 shallot, finely chopped	30ml/1fl oz red wine
1 tablespoon freshly chopped thyme	55g/2oz rocket leaves
1 garlic clove, chopped	1 teaspoon balsamic vinegar

Heat two of the tablespoons of oil in a frying pan and fry the shallot, thyme and garlic for 3 minutes. Add the rabbit livers and cook for a further 4 minutes. Add the wine, and then remove the pan from the hob.

Toss the rocket leaves with the remaining tablespoon of oil and balsamic vinegar, and arrange on top of the bruschetta slices. Place a spoonful of the rabbit liver mixture on top, and serve immediately.

Rabbit in Champagne

In the introduction to *The Rabbit Cook* you might recall that there was some discussion as to whether or not real champagne was required for this recipe. The general consensus of opinion was that it was not, and that any type of sparkling wine would do (or even ordinary white wine) – so keep the champagne for drinking whilst you prepare this dish!

Olive oil, enough to sauté the vegetables
1 large onion, roughly chopped
1 stick celery, roughly chopped
1 leek, roughly chopped
1 clove garlic, crushed
A little flour, for dusting the meat
2 small rabbits, jointed

300ml/10fl oz sparkling white wine or Cava
1 tablespoon French mustard
Bouquet garni
Pinch of thyme
Seasoning
1 dessertspoon double cream
Chopped flat-leaf parsley and croûtons

Heat some oil and sauté the vegetables and garlic, then place them in a casserole dish.

Put the flour into a polythene bag, add the rabbit joints, and shake well until all the joints are coated. Remove them, and cook in a frying pan until each joint is sealed; then transfer them to a casserole dish. Deglaze the frying pan with the wine, and add to the casserole together with the mustard, bouquet garni, thyme, double cream and seasoning.

Cook at gas mark 4/180°C for around 30 minutes.

To serve, remove the rabbit pieces, reduce the sauce, and garnish with chopped flat-leaf parsley and croûtons.

'FRYER' RABBIT

The term 'fryer' generally refers to a young rabbit weighing not less than 700g/1½lb and almost never more than 1.5kg/3½lb. The flesh is tender and fine-grained, and is just right for the following simple frying technique.

Cut the rabbit into serving-sized pieces, and together with a chilli pepper and about four peeled and sliced cloves of garlic, parboil it in just enough water to cover the rabbit pieces. When the rabbit is heading towards being tender, remove it from the water with a slotted spoon.

Take 250ml/8fl oz milk and two slightly beaten eggs, and mix them in a bowl. Dip the rabbit pieces into the milk/egg mix, and then dust them with plain flour into which a little seasoning has been added. One of the easiest ways to do this is to place the flour and meat into a plastic bag and shake it until the rabbit pieces are thoroughly coated.

Fry the rabbit in a deep frying pan into which a generous knob of butter (or lard) has been added.

Pressure-Cooked Blanquette of Rabbit

Correctly used, a pressure cooker is economical and can produce some excellent quality meals that can be ready in no more than a third of the normal cooking time. Does anyone still use their pressure cooker these days? If so, try this method and have a meal ready in less than half an hour.

1 rabbit, jointed	2 tablespoons butter
300ml/10fl oz chicken stock	2 tablespoons flour
2 medium onions, sliced	300ml/10fl oz milk
2–3 cloves	1 egg yolk
Bouquet garni	2 tablespoons cream
Strip of lemon peel	2 tablespoons cooked chopped ham
1 rabbit, jointed	Parsley and slices of lemon for garnish

Lift the trivet from the pressure cooker, put in the stock, the sliced onions, seasonings and rabbit joints. Bring to pressure in the usual way, cook for the required time, and reduce the pressure with cold water.

During cooking, make the sauce with the butter, flour and milk. Lift out the rabbit and keep hot in a casserole dish. Strain the stock and add sufficient of the sauce to give a coating consistency. Reheat, taste, and correct the seasoning if necessary.

Add the mixed cream and egg yolk and cook again, but without reboiling. Pour over the rabbit joints, and garnish with the chopped ham, parsley and lemon slices.

'Blanquettes' are usually served with plain white rice or boiled new potatoes.

Plating up a rabbit dish at The Boar's Head, Ripley, North Yorkshire.

Trimmings and Accompaniments

When planning a meal for guests, it is as well to try and imagine exactly how the colours of all the combined ingredients will appear to them once on a serving plate. For the same reason, take some time choosing the crockery to best suit your intended menu, as too rich and deep a pattern can swamp the colours of the meal. Of course, it is not possible or practicable to have a different set of plates to compliment every single recipe, but it is, nevertheless, a general point worth bearing in mind. Size matters, too: a vast array of food cramped on a small plate can be overbearing and is certainly not as visually attractive – no matter how spectacular its contents are to taste! Big and plain seems to be the order of the day as far as choosing plates most suitable for the rabbit cook.

It has been mentioned elsewhere just how well autumnal fruits and winter vegetables go with many rabbit dishes: the dark hues of a blackberry- or damson-based sauce can look fantastic when set against the vibrancy of roasted vegetables such as squash, carrots and swede – and if all else fails, a spoonful of beautifully green garden peas will always give any main course that all-important visual 'lift'.

Many of the recipes in this book start with similar preparation instructions, namely that the rabbit is jointed and then, in a frying pan, either sealed prior to being placed in the oven, or cooked slowly on the hob. Vegetables – notably onions, carrots, leeks, celery and garlic – are often included, and so, given this regular approach, what can make each finished dish different and exciting? The answer must be the subtle nuances – the inclusion of nuts, herbs, lemon zest and even honey – but above all, it is probably the sauces that accompany each dish: these transform something ordinary into something extraordinary. The way these are made is often covered alongside the recipe itself, and so there is no need to add any extra ones here. What we have done, though, is to include in this chapter just a few trimmings and accompaniments that we know work well with rabbit.

The way a sauce is made will transform a moderate dish into an outstanding one.

VEGETABLES

Some rabbit recipes that include a sauce do not need any additional flavours added and it would be a shame to confuse the taste buds by incorporating extra – and totally unnecessary – sauces to any vegetable dishes served with them. Steamed and *al dente*, the traditional seasonal types such as potatoes, carrots, cauliflower, broccoli, peas, beans, leeks, spinach and asparagus are generally all that are needed to accompany a carefully prepared main course; however, on occasions where something a little different is required, or when imagination is lacking after a busy day, some of the following suggestions may be of assistance.

Roasted Ratatouille

No sooner have we discussed at reasonable length that most rabbit dishes will be eaten during the autumn and winter months and will therefore be accompanied most advantageously by vegetables sourced during those particular seasons, than we contradict ourselves by suggesting that this recipe is perfect for the summer! In fact, if you like, you can bundle everything together into a foil parcel and place it directly on a barbecue grill; otherwise use a conventional oven.

1 large aubergine, cut into chunks	2 large tomatoes, chopped
1 red onion, thinly sliced	1 garlic clove, crushed
2 courgettes, cut into rounds	2 tablespoons olive oil
2 orange or yellow peppers, cut into strips	Fresh basil leaves for garnish

On a large piece of double thickness kitchen foil laid on a baking tray, place all the ingredients. Mix the oil together with the crushed garlic and drizzle over. Fold together the sides of the foil until a parcel is formed and cook in a hot oven (or over barbecue ashes!) for about 30 minutes, opening and turning halfway through cooking with the aid of a spatula.

Unwrap and sprinkle with freshly torn basil leaves before taking to the table.

Roasted Shallots and Squash

Perfect with almost any rabbit dish, this is particularly delicious when served with rice rather than potatoes.

60ml/2fl oz olive oil	1 teaspoon fresh thyme, finely chopped
15ml/½fl oz balsamic vinegar	15g/½oz flat leaf parsley
15ml/½fl oz sweet soy sauce	1–2 small garlic cloves, finely chopped
Salt and pepper for seasoning	75g/2¾oz chopped walnuts
350g/12oz whole shallots, peeled	150g/5½oz Feta cheese
3 fresh red chillies	
1 butternut squash, peeled, deseeded and cut into chunks	

In a bowl, mix together the olive oil, balsamic vinegar and soy sauce and season with salt and pepper. Toss the shallots and two of the chillies into the mixture and then place all into an ovenproof dish or roasting tin.

Roast at gas mark 6/200°C for about a quarter of an hour, then add the butternut squash chunks and roast for a further half hour, or until the squash is browned and tender. Remove from the oven and stir in the thyme.

Chop the parsley and garlic together and mix with the walnuts, and stir them into the roasted vegetables.

Deseed the last chilli (taking care to avoid getting any part of it on to your skin or in your eyes), chop it very finely and add it to the vegetables.

Finally, crumble the cheese over, transfer to a serving dish, and take immediately to the table.

Roasted Shallots and Squash.

Parsnip and Apple Mash

Parsnip and apple mash makes a delicious change from conventional mashed potato.

750g/1lb 10oz Maris Piper potatoes
225g/8oz parsnips
1 large eating apple, peeled, cored
   and cubed

2 tablespoons of crème fraîche
2 tablespoons each of chopped fresh parsley
   and chopped fresh chives

Peel the potatoes and parsnips. Cut them into even-sized chunks and boil in two separate pans for 15–20 minutes until tender; add the apple cubes to the parsnip pan for the final 5 minutes.

Drain both pans well, then add the parsnips to the potatoes and stir over a low heat just long enough to drive off any moisture still remaining.

Remove from the heat, mash with butter in the normal way, and then blend in the crème fraîche and parsley and fresh chives. Keep hot until ready to serve.

Parsnips in Batter

Like 'Parsnip and Apple Mash', parsnips in batter make a change from the normal – and you get to combine your veggies with a sort of Yorkshire pudding!

4–6 parsnips, peeled and cut into small chunks
30g/1oz fat

1 dessertspoon clear, runny honey

For the batter
150g/5½oz plain flour
300ml/10fl oz milk
2 eggs

A little salt and pepper to season
Pinch of dried mustard powder

Discard any particularly 'woody' sections of the parsnips before cutting them into chunks and blanching in boiling water for 1–2 minutes. Dry, and toss them in a frying pan to which the fat and honey have been added. Turn frequently, making sure that all sides of the parsnips have been coated.

Grease ten to twelve patty tins, then make the batter as follows:

Sieve the flour into a bowl and add salt and pepper plus a pinch of mustard. Make a well in the centre, and add two eggs and the milk: then beat thoroughly until a smooth batter is achieved.

Divide the parsnips into the patty tins, pour on the batter, and bake for 15–20 minutes at gas mark 7/220°C.

Turnip and Tarragon Rosti

This makes a perfect accompaniment to almost any rabbit dish – or in fact, any game-textured meat.

285g/10oz turnip, peeled and grated
140g/5oz potatoes, peeled and grated
14g/½oz chopped tarragon

Salt and pepper, to taste
55g/2oz butter
1 tablespoon olive oil

Peel the turnip and potatoes, and grate on the largest holes of your grater. Mix both together in a bowl and stir in the chopped tarragon, together with a generous pinch of seasoning.

In a heavy-bottomed frying pan (it needs to go in the oven, so make sure it is 'fit for purpose'), heat the butter and olive oil until the butter is frothing, and swirl it around the pan; then lay in the grated mixture and firm it down (gently) with either a palette knife or the back of a wooden spoon. Cook on a medium heat for about 10 minutes (with a lid on), occasionally working round the edges of the frying pan with a knife, or until you see the edges beginning to brown.

Lightly oil a plate big enough to hold the rosti; hold it over the pan, flip the pan over, and then slide the rosti back into the pan so that the browned side is now facing upwards.

Return to the heat for a further 5–10 minutes (without a lid this time), then put it on the bottom of a pre-heated oven, gas mark 7/220°C, for about half an hour.

Rondle Wood Rosti

Philip's wife Tricia is a dab hand when it comes to preparing this particular rosti, which she often cooks at their delightful Rondle Wood country cottage.

750g/1lb10oz medium sized potatoes
1½ tablespoons olive oil ('Ideally, not "extra virgin",' says Tricia)
55g/2oz butter

1 medium-sized onion
55g/2oz grated cheese
Parsley, as garnish

Boil the whole unpeeled potatoes for 10 minutes, then peel and coarsely grate them once cold. Lightly fry the onions. Add these and the cheese to the mixture, season and then heat the butter and oil together in a 23cm/9in frying pan.

Add the potato mixture, level off the top and fry for 10 minutes on a medium heat. Have a flattish plate ready, and at the end of the cooking time, invert the potatoes on to this: return the rosti to the pan the other way up. Fry for a further 10 minutes, by which time both sides should be golden brown. Place on the table, garnished with parsley on top and serve in individual slices.

A rosti of any kind makes the perfect accompaniment.

BUBBLE AND SQUEAK

For some reason, good old 'bubble and squeak' goes well with rabbit. Mash your boiled potatoes with a little butter, but do not add any milk or cream as you perhaps would normally. Quickly boil some chopped cabbage or Brussels sprouts until they are cooked but still recognizably green (as 'bubble and squeak' is a traditional method of using up leftovers, cold vegetables from a previous meal will do), and drain well.

Fry two large onions in 30g/1oz butter until they are soft yet not discoloured, and add them to the mashed potatoes, together with the greens.

Reheat your frying pan and add a further 30g/1oz butter. Tip in the bubble and squeak mix, flatten into a rough pancake shape, and fry for a couple of minutes, or until the base is golden brown; then turn, and repeat the process on the other side (to turn the mix over, use the plate method as described for 'Turnip and Tarragon Rosti', see above, page 71).

'Spring Onion Potato Cakes'

To make spring onion potato cakes follow the above principles, but use a large bunch of finely chopped spring onions in place of the two onions, and omit the cabbage or Brussels sprouts. All potato cakes should be dusted with a little flour before being pan-fried. Once cooked, the cakes can be set to one side, and baked in the oven when required.

Pommes Boulangère

Basically these are *Dauphinoise* potatoes by another name; either will go well with many of the rabbit dishes featured here. The idea of including it here comes from one of Jeremy's French neighbours, who seems to serve a similar dish at almost every meal to which he's ever been invited – so much so that she has now become known in the Hobson household as 'Madame Dauphinoise'!

100g/3½oz butter
225g/8oz onions, sliced
1 sprig thyme
1 clove garlic, chopped

2 sprigs parsley
1kg/2¼lb potatoes, cut into thin slices
1.5ltr/3 pints chicken or vegetable stock

Using roughly half of the butter, sweat the onions, thyme and garlic in a heavy-bottomed pan. Finely chop the parsley sprigs into the onion mix, then take the pan off the heat.

In the bottom of a shallow (about 5cm/2in deep) ovenproof dish, arrange a layer of the sliced potatoes, then spread half the onion mix over. Add another layer of potatoes, and then a second layer of onion. Finally top off with more potato.

Heat the stock and pour it gently into the dish; spread the remaining butter randomly over the potato topping and place in the oven for about an hour at gas mark 5/190°C.

The potatoes should be soft when speared with the point of a sharp knife, and the top layer should be golden in colour.

Bacon and Brussels Sprouts

Bacon goes well with rabbit, as do Brussels sprouts, so it seemed a good idea to put the two together. We've seen sprouts cooked in the normal way and then bacon strips or lardons added at the last minute – but then you still have the tedious job of peeling the outer layers of each sprout and inserting that all-important 'cross' at its base. And after all that time and effort, such is the reputation of sprouts that the majority go cold and untouched in the serving dish! But try them this way and your guests will find it difficult to refuse – and you will save yourself preparation time into the bargain. As Shirley Conran once famously said, 'Life's too short to stuff a mushroom': well, we think the same regarding preparing sprouts!

30g/1oz butter
100g/3½oz streaky bacon, cut into
  'lardons'

450g/1lb Brussels sprouts, shredded
  (either with a knife or in a food processor)
Salt and pepper

In a shallow pan, heat the butter and fry the bacon pieces until they are heading towards being crisp. Add the shredded sprouts, season and mix or shake together, and cook until they have picked up a glossy coating from all the bacon juices and butter. Some should look slightly golden brown.

Game Chips

You cannot possibly have a cookery book that deals with rabbit without including a recipe for game chips.

700g/1½lb potatoes
Vegetable oil (quantities depend on whether a chip pan or a deep frying pan is used)

Peel and slice (very thinly) the potatoes. Place them in a colander and run the cold tap over them in order to remove any excess starch; then dry the slices on kitchen roll.

Heat some oil in a chip pan and add the potatoes, a few slices at a time. Fry until crisp and golden brown.

Once done, remove any excess fat by placing the chips on more kitchen roll. Then place them in the bottom of a reasonably hot oven to keep them warm until ready for serving.

Fennel and Borlotti Bean Bake

This is a very tasty combination that goes extremely well with many rabbit dishes, especially those that have their origins in Italy. The recipe is taken from *The Olive Oil*

Cookbook written by Louise Pickford (Salamander Books – itself an imprint of Anova Books, London – 1994).

115g/4oz tinned borlotti beans	150ml/5fl oz dry white wine
100ml/3½fl oz olive oil	450g/1lb tinned plum tomatoes, drained
4 small head of fennel, cut into thin slices	55g/2oz of tinned anchovies, drained of all oil
1 onion, thinly sliced	55g/2oz olives, pitted and chopped
2 cloves garlic, chopped	30g/1oz capers
1 tablespoon each of freshly chopped	450g/1lb cooked, sliced potatoes
rosemary and thyme	55g/2oz Gruyère cheese
	Salt and pepper

Whilst boiling the potatoes, cook the borlotti beans following the instructions on the tin. Put the oil in a frying pan and fry the fennel slices for 5 minutes or until golden in colour. Remove from the pan and leave to one side whilst you fry the onion, garlic and herbs for 5 minutes.

Add the wine and boil rapidly, then stir in the tomatoes and return the fennel to the pan. Cover and simmer for quarter of an hour. Season, and stir in all the remaining ingredients, with the exception of the potato slices and cheese.

Add the beans, and spoon all into a casserole dish. Top with the potato slices and grate over the cheese (use Cheddar if you prefer). Bake for half an hour at gas mark 6/200°C.

Cheese Potato Bakes

To you and me these are basically baked jacket potatoes, but they are done with a twist to their preparation and make an interesting and slightly different accompanying vegetable to a rabbit casserole.

8 evenly sized potatoes	Pinch of grated nutmeg
50g/1¾oz butter	Salt and pepper
Half a soupspoon chopped parsley	30g/1oz Gruyère cheese

Wash the potatoes and cut the skins all the way round so that each potato has a 'lid'. Thickly coat them with salt and cook in a moderate oven, gas mark 6/200°C for about three-quarters of an hour.

Take off the lids (and keep them warm) and empty the potatoes without damaging the skin 'shells'. Mix the potato with the parsley, nutmeg, and salt and pepper. Fill the skins with the mixture, and grate over the cheese, then place them back in the oven for a further 15 minutes.

Replace the lids and serve in a deep dish.

Cheese potato bakes.

SEARED CHANTERELLE MUSHROOMS

Strong-tasting mushrooms go well with many rabbit dishes: chanterelles are ideal, as are black trompettes. To maintain the taste of any type of mushroom it is essential to brown the outside and seal in the flavour; this is best achieved by placing just enough mushrooms to cover the bottom of a pan, into which a very small knob of butter has been added, and cooking them over a medium-high heat for a matter of minutes. Cooking them over too low a heat will allow the mushrooms to 'sweat' and lose their all-important moisture.

Note: Keep mushrooms stored in a brown paper bag and *not* in a plastic bag in the fridge.

Cheesy Artichokes

Not quite cauliflower cheese, this recipe is nevertheless a cheese-flavoured vegetable dish that features an interesting use of artichokes. In fact, it's a sort of artichoke Welsh rarebit for rabbit! However, a word of warning: do not use it if the rabbit recipe you have chosen already incorporates another type of sauce, because the strength of the cheese will probably nullify the subtleties and nuances of the other, far more important, sauce that the recipe suggests.

8 artichokes

2 lemons

1 bowl of water containing the juice of 2 further lemons

1ltr/1¾ pints game stock (*see* page 84)

For the cheese sauce

250g/9oz Collier's Welsh Cheddar cheese (or any strong Cheddar)

30g/1oz butter

100ml/3½fl oz milk

½ teaspoon dry mustard powder

½ teaspoon cayenne pepper

Worcestershire sauce, a 'dash' of

Salt and pepper

Prepare the artichokes by cutting the hearts from the stalks; remove the outer 'leaves' from the hearts, and then squeeze the juice of two lemons over the hearts, rubbing them well with the juice to prevent them from turning black.

Prepare one heart at a time, dropping it into the bowl of cold water and lemon juice as you go. Stir occasionally.

Then drain the hearts and cook them in just enough game stock to cover them. Use a pan for this. The actual cooking time will vary, but they should be cooked until the hairy 'choke' part is easily removed from the heart.

Remove the hairy part with a spoon, discard, and place the prepared hearts in a greased baking dish.

For the sauce, melt the cheese and butter in the milk in a pan over a gentle heat. Then add the mustard, pepper, a pinch of salt and a dash of Worcestershire sauce. Spoon some of the resultant mixture into each of the artichoke hearts, sprinkle over the cayenne pepper and cook them in the oven at gas mark 9/240°C for a quarter of an hour.

Serve immediately alongside your chosen rabbit recipe.

Winter vegetables can really add to the enjoyment of a cold-weather recipe for rabbit.

Vegetable Soufflé

This can be used with any green vegetable rather than the peas included here. The soufflé can be served on its own, but it goes exceptionally well alongside young fried rabbit (see page 65).

1 small onion, peeled and chopped	150ml/5fl oz milk (warmed)
55g/2oz butter	55g/2oz ham, cut into small strips
1.25kg/2lb 12oz peas	30g/1oz grated cheese
Salt	3 eggs, separated and the whites stiffly beaten
1 tablespoon flour	

Fry the onion in half the butter, and add the peas. Pour boiling water over them, season with salt, and cook until the peas are tender. Pass through a sieve.

In a separate pan, melt the remainder of the butter and make a roux by adding the flour and stirring vigorously. Add the warmed milk slowly, stirring all the time. Put the ham and the grated cheese into the sauce. Mix in the sieved peas. Add the egg yolks and the stiffly beaten egg whites.

Pour the mixture into a buttered cake tin or soufflé dish, cover the top with greaseproof paper, and steam for 1 hour.

Mushroom and Green Bean Risotto

Another of Philip's 'signature' dishes, we know this works every time, and although we've not tried it alongside a rabbit recipe, we have no reason to doubt that it would 'marry' with almost any of the suggestions given in Chapter 2.

75g/2¾oz green beans (haricots verts)	300g/10½oz Arborio rice
100g/3½oz field mushrooms	1 small glass of white wine
A little olive oil	1ltr/1¾ pint stock – vegetable, game or
1 medium-sized onion	chicken
55g/2oz butter	

Boil the beans for 5 minutes, and then run cold water over them to stop them cooking further. Put to one side for the time being.

Lightly fry the sliced mushrooms in a little olive oil until just cooked. Put aside.

Fry the sliced onion in the butter until the onion is soft but not brown. Add the rice and stir briefly so as to coat the rice. Then pour the wine over and simmer for 2 to 3 minutes, stirring all the time.

The risotto will now take about 20 minutes to cook: slowly add the stock, and about halfway through the cooking time, incorporate the beans and mushrooms.

When the risotto is ready, the water should have been absorbed, but the risotto should still be moist, with the rice continuing to be a little al dente.

Mushroom and Green Bean Risotto.

DUMPLINGS

All stews and casseroles benefit from the inclusion of dumplings of one sort or another. They might not be the healthiest of accompaniment, but on a cold winter's evening they are definitely the best! One or two of the recipes have included a specific type of dumpling (the one supplied by Kinga McArdle – see page 22 – springs immediately to mind), but others can have any of the following added half an hour or so before the recommended cooking time is completed.

Nockerl (Hungarian Dumplings)

Nockerl are famously served with goulash, and as such should be made and used in conjunction with the 'Rabbit Goulash' recipe on page 44.

225g/8oz plain flour
Salt
2 eggs

85g/3oz melted butter
Water (with which to make the dough)

Put the flour and salt into a mixing bowl, make a well in the centre, break in the eggs, and stir carefully so as to draw the flour into the eggs. Add the melted butter and the water as required.

Leave the dough in a cold place for half an hour before cutting out teaspoons of the mixture with a hot spoon. Rinse them under cold water and cook them without browning in either butter or beef dripping.

Bread Dumplings

Dumplings of any kind are always good with rabbit casserole, and together make the ideal winter 'comfort' food. Bread dumplings are a little different to the normal suet variety and are easily made.

1 tablespoon finely chopped onion	2 eggs
2 tablespoons softened butter	½ cup of cracker biscuit crumbs
2 cups wholewheat breadcrumbs, soaked	1 teaspoon chopped parsley
in water and squeezed dry	Pinch each of paprika, nutmeg and ginger
1 teaspoon salt	

In a saucepan, sauté the chopped onion in the butter until golden. Stir in the bread-crumbs together with a teaspoon of salt.

Remove the pan from the heat, and cool the mixture. Stir in the eggs, cracker biscuit crumbs, parsley and the pinch each of paprika, nutmeg and ginger, stirring well. Shape the mixture into balls and add to the rabbit casserole for the last 15–20 minutes of its scheduled cooking time. If the mixture is too crumbly to shape, add a few drops of water or olive oil.

Bread Mushroom Dumplings

225g/8oz mushrooms, finely chopped	2 tablespoons chopped fresh parsley
1 onion, finely chopped	1 dessertspoon tomato purée
A little olive oil for frying	1 beaten egg
115g/4oz white breadcrumbs	Flour, for rolling

Lightly fry the mushrooms with the onion in the olive oil, then mix them in a bowl with the breadcrumbs, parsley, tomato purée and egg. Bind the mixture together well, then shape it into small balls (if you use about a tablespoon of mixture for each ball, you should end up with between twelve and fourteen miniature dumplings).

Coat each one with flour, then brown in hot oil in a frying pan. When well seared, add to the stew or casserole for the last 20–30 minutes of cooking.

Cheesy Nettle Potato Dumplings

Nettles are the 'in' thing in modern cooking; young ones make an unusual alternative to spinach as an accompaniment to many dishes, including rabbit, and at least two of our main rabbit recipes describe their use. 'Cheesy Nettle Potato Dumplings' are a little unusual but well worth considering!

450g/1lb nettle leaves	Salt and pepper, for seasoning
1.3kg/3lb potatoes, peeled and quartered	225g/8oz flour
2 eggs	30g/1oz butter
½ teaspoon grated nutmeg	

For the cheesy sauce
200g/7oz Cheddar cheese
60ml/2fl oz milk

Blanch, drain and chop the nettle leaves. Cook the potatoes in a pan of boiling water until they are tender; mash until they are creamy.

In a bowl, mix together the mashed potatoes, eggs, nutmeg and seasoning, then add the nettle leaves and fold all gently together. Add the flour a little at a time until a dough consistency is formed (it should eventually form a large, barely sticky ball).

On a floured board, roll segments of the dough ball into smaller dumpling shapes about 2.45cm (1in) in diameter. Cook by dropping the dumplings into boiling salted water until they rise to the surface. Strain and toss with butter.

At the very last minute make the sauce by melting the cheese over a gentle heat and adding milk until a thick, creamy consistency is achieved. Pour over the nettle potato dumplings, and serve immediately.

STUFFINGS

Like a dog, stuffings are not just for Christmas! They are perfect when actually stuffed into the body cavity of a rabbit, or when made and served as a side dish. It is worth remembering that a stuffing shouldn't be too wet, otherwise it will become stodgy, nor too dry or it will not 'bind' together well. Traditionally, most stuffings involve a base of breadcrumbs, but sometimes rice or suet can be used with great success.

Anchovy Stuffing

Anchovies: love them or hate them! This stuffing recipe has its origins in Italy.

55g/2oz breadcrumbs
12 black olives, stoned and chopped
6 anchovy fillets, chopped
30g/1oz sultanas
1 teaspoon capers

1 clove garlic, chopped
A little fresh parsley, chopped
1 teaspoon olive oil
Salt and pepper

Mix together all the ingredients, moisten with olive oil, and season with salt and pepper.

Simple Olive and Bread Stuffing

A perfect, simple and tasty stuffing recipe suitable for rabbit and pigeon (and much more besides!).

100g/3½oz bread (be as adventurous as you like as regards type)
30g/1oz black olives, stoned and roughly chopped
2 tablespoons fresh parsley, roughly chopped
Lemon zest

55g/2oz fresh mozzarella, cut and cubed
2 tablespoons olive oil
30g/1oz butter
½ medium-sized onion, peeled and finely chopped
1 clove garlic, finely chopped
Salt and pepper to season

Dry the bread in a low oven, and then grate or place in a food processor to make crumbs. Put the crumbs in a mixing bowl, and add the olives, parsley, lemon zest and mozzarella.

Heat the oil and butter, and sauté the onion and garlic until they are soft. Cool and add to the ingredients already in the bowl. Season to taste.

Use according to the instructions for whatever recipe is chosen. Alternatively, if you are going to use it as a side dish, put it in a baking tray at a high heat until the top has gone slightly crusty.

Spinach and Mushroom Stuffing

Try this recipe with roast rabbit. The fact that it is served in triangular cake-like wedges makes it an interesting and unusual accompaniment.

1 large onion, chopped
2 tablespoons olive oil
140g/5oz mushrooms
225g/8oz young spinach leaves

115g/4oz freshly grated breadcrumbs
Salt and pepper to season
100g/3½oz Cheddar cheese

Heat one tablespoon of the oil in a heavy-bottomed pan and add the chopped onion; cover and cook for about 15 minutes, or until the onion is soft.

Roughly slice the mushrooms – as regards type, be as adventurous as you like with whatever is available from the greengrocers (unless you are absolutely positive of a correct identification, it is dangerous to risk using anything picked from the wild); add them to the onion base, and fry for 2–3 minutes. Then add the spinach leaves: cook only until they begin to wilt. Add the freshly grated breadcrumbs and seasoning, and mix well.

Heat the remainder of the oil in a small, non-stick frying pan and put the stuffing mix into this, pressing it down firmly (use a wooden spoon) so that the mixture forms a thick pancake. Fry the underside until it is crisp and golden coloured.

Remove from the hob and grate a thin layer of cheese over the top, then place the pan under the grill for a few minutes in order to brown off the top.

Turn out on to a plate, and cut into wedges.

Spinach and Mushroom Stuffing.

Apple Stuffing

Originally this very old recipe for apple stuffing was made with fat salt pork: in the interests of health and modern thinking we have substituted streaky bacon, which is not much better but at least we try!

115g/4oz streaky bacon, very finely chopped
1 stick celery, chopped
1 onion, chopped
5 cooking apples, peeled and chopped

2 tablespoons parsley
115g/4oz sugar
115g/4oz breadcrumbs
Seasoning

Place the bacon pieces into a pan and cook. Add the celery and onion, and cook for 3 minutes. Add the apples, parsley and sugar. Put a lid on the pan and cook for 20 minutes, then cook without the lid until any remaining liquid is reduced. Add the breadcrumbs, and season with salt and pepper.

Use in the usual way.

Chestnut Purée

A chestnut stuffing or purée is a common 'trimming' for many game dishes, including those containing rabbit.

700g/1½lb chestnuts
50g/1¾oz celeriac, chopped
250ml/8fl oz milk

100ml/3½fl oz fresh cream
Salt and pepper

Peel the chestnuts and put them into boiling water to remove their skins, then cook them with the celeriac in lightly salted water for about 45 minutes. Strain and press through a sieve.

Boil the milk, and then gently add both the milk and the cream to the purée until the desired consistency is reached. Add seasoning before serving. Serve in a dish.

GAME AND BROWN STOCK

Several of the recipes outlined in *The Rabbit Cook* recommend the use of a game-based stock or similar. Like the making of marinades, quantities of liquids and varieties of ingredients can be altered to suit, so don't be afraid to adapt any of the suggestions that follow.

Game Stock

Game stock can be made from the fresh carcasses of game birds or rabbits from which the meat has been removed for another recipe; or if you have had a roast rabbit or game bird, the left-over carcasses could be used. Giblets can also be included.

Place two rabbit or pheasant carcasses in a heavy-bottomed pan, and add the following ingredients:

Half a garlic bulb, roughly crushed	3 bay leaves
3–4 sticks of celery	3 sprigs each of fresh thyme, rosemary and
2 small leeks	parsley
2 small onions	4–5 black peppercorns
2 medium-sized carrots	Approximately 4.5ltr/8 pints cold water
(all the vegetables should be roughly	
chopped)	

Bring to the boil, then reduce the heat and simmer gently for about 4 hours, skimming off the fat as it appears. Once the process is complete, pour the stock through a fine sieve into storage containers.

Brown Stock

If you can get hold of some beef bones, place them in a roasting tray or similar together with a couple of sliced onions and carrots; brown the bones on all sides in a moderately hot oven. Transfer all to a large, heavy-bottomed pan and add the following:

About 3.5ltr/6 pints water	A bouquet garni
½ tablespoon salt	A couple of celery stalks
A pinch of thyme	

Bring to the boil, then turn down the heat and simmer for about 4 hours, or until the stock has reduced by about a third. Skim off any accumulating fat as and when necessary throughout this period – use a large spoon, or soak it up with kitchen roll; alternatively, let the stock cool completely when it will form a 'crust', which can be lifted off.

Finally, strain the liquid through a sieve into storage containers.

Store in the fridge (for up to a week), or freeze (for two to three months) ready to use in a brown sauce.

SUITABLE SALADS

Salads make the perfect accompaniment for many rabbit dishes, especially those that are barbecued, such as the 'Barbecued Rabbit with Saffron and Yoghurt', as described on page 62. It must be admitted, however, that a summer-type salad that might go well with a pigeon-inspired dish, for instance, generally hasn't the 'power' to add anything at all to a meaty rabbit recipe.

Pleasant though it is to look at, a summer-type salad that might go well on other occasions generally hasn't the 'power' to add anything at all to a meaty rabbit recipe.

Char-Grilled Vegetable Quinoa Salad

1 red pepper, deseeded and sliced
1 yellow pepper, deseeded and sliced
1 courgette, sliced
1 red onion, peeled and sliced
3 tablespoons olive oil

Salt and pepper to season
225g/8oz quinoa
500ml/18fl oz water
1 small lemon, zested and juiced
30g/1oz fresh flat-leaved parsley, roughly
     chopped

Toss the peppers, courgette and onion in two tablespoons of olive oil together with a little seasoning. Over a medium heat, barbecue them for 6–8 minutes, turning frequently until they are slightly browned.

At the same time boil the water, add the quinoa, and cover and simmer for about 10 minutes, or as according to the instructions on the quinoa packet. After making sure that all the water has been absorbed, set aside for a few minutes before finally tipping the quinoa into a serving bowl.

Add the char-grilled vegetables and the remaining spoonful of olive oil. Incorporate the juice and zest of the lemon, together with the chopped parsley, and gently fold before serving.

Chicory and Bacon Salad

In France this recipe is known as '*Salade de pissenlits au lard*', due to the fact that it was traditionally made from dandelion shoots that had been blanched by being grown under flowerpots (in much the same way as rhubarb crowns are forced by being grown under buckets or upturned dustbins). The French would always mix this salad at the last minute when everyone was sitting at the table.

2 heads of chicory
2 tablespoons wine vinegar
225g/8oz streaky bacon, diced
    (or use lardons if preferred)

A little goose or bacon fat
1 hardboiled egg, chopped

Prepare the heads of chicory by washing them in plenty of water in order to remove any dirt and grit. Remove the bottom, retaining only the palest of the leaves. Rub a wooden salad bowl with a piece of cut garlic clove, add the chicory leaves and sprinkle over the wine vinegar.

Fry the bacon pieces in a little of the fat for about 5 minutes, then pour both the bacon and fat into the salad. Finally garnish with the hardboiled egg.

Beetroot and Red Onion Salad

Normally recommended for use with roast beef, there is no reason at all why this salad should not go well with either rabbit or pigeon (for some delicious pigeon recipes, look out for *The Pigeon Cook* written by ourselves and also published by The Crowood Press).

500g/1¼lb small beetroot, precooked and sliced

60ml/2fl oz olive oil

90g/3oz walnuts

1 teaspoon caster sugar

Salt and pepper

30ml/1fl oz walnut oil

1 tablespoon balsamic vinegar

1 teaspoon soy sauce

1 teaspoon grated orange rind

½ teaspoon ground and dry roasted coriander seeds*

2 teaspoons orange juice

1 red onion, peeled, halved and finely sliced

2 tablespoons fresh fennel, chopped

A handful each of fresh watercress and washed beetroot leaves

Toss the beetroot slices in a little of the olive oil. Heat a little more of the oil in a small frying pan, and cook the walnuts until they begin to brown. Add the sugar and stir until the walnuts look to be caramelizing. Season with the salt and pepper, then tip them on to a plate to cool.

In a bowl, mix together the remaining olive oil, the walnut oil, balsamic vinegar, soy sauce, orange rind and juice, and the coriander.

Place the beetroot and onion slices into a large bowl and add the dressing as made above. Make a salad of the fennel, watercress and beetroot leaves and sprinkle with the walnuts. Serve the salad and the beetroot/onion mix in two separate bowls.

A selection of nuts and croûtons that are often used in salads.

* Note: To dry roast any type of nuts or seeds, simply place them in a small frying pan (to which no oil has been added). Their natural oils will be sufficient to roast or toast the nuts and seeds in just a minute or two.

Italian Salad

In Italy this salad is almost always used with rabbit – which has generally been marinated and cooked in a large pan of water, vinegar and wine before being stripped from the bone and served alongside this filling dish.

300g/10½oz Bulgar wheat
1ltr/1¾ pints water
150g/5½oz each of fresh broad beans,
   cannelloni beans and borlotti beans
150g/5½oz tender fresh peas (or frozen
   petit pois)

1 cucumber, deseeded, sliced and cut into
   quarters
Juice of a lemon
Sea salt and freshly ground black pepper for
   seasoning

Place the wheat into a large saucepan, add the water and simmer until the wheat is tender. Drain and leave to cool.

   Rinse out the pan and use it to cook the three bean types and the peas in boiling, salted water for about 5 minutes; then drain.

Italian Salad.

Mix together the wheat, beans, peas, cucumber pieces and the lemon juice. Season and serve immediately.

Arabian Salad

Simple to make, the freshness of the oranges will enhance the flavour of rabbit.

3 oranges, peeled and sliced thinly
2 medium onions, sliced thinly
115g/4oz black olives, stoned

2 tablespoons extra virgin olive oil
Sea salt and freshly ground black pepper to
season

Mix all the ingredients together, and season with salt and pepper.

PICKLES AND CHUTNEYS

Living in the rural countryside, 'Granny' quite often did know best when it came to preserving summer and autumn produce in order that they could be safely eaten along-side other easily obtainable ingredients all the year round. It is no surprise, then, that many pickles and chutneys go very well with a variety of rabbit dishes. We have written a book containing over 100 pickles, chutneys and relishes, several of which would be perfect accompaniments to the main recipes contained within these pages, so we thought it might be useful to include just five of them here (*Making Traditional and Modern Chutneys, Pickles and Relishes*, The Crowood Press, 2010).

Pear and Apple Chutney

Laurence Murphy of 'Fat Olives', Emsworth, Hampshire, kindly gave us this recipe.

6 firm Conference pears, peeled, cored and diced
2 Bramley apples, peeled, cored and diced
2 onions, finely chopped
½ teaspoon ground nutmeg
1 tablespoon pink peppercorns
225g/8oz castor sugar

1 tablespoon black treacle
3 cloves
1 bay leaf
125ml/4fl oz balsamic vinegar
Salt and pepper

Place all the ingredients into a large, heavy-bottomed pan over a low heat and cook slowly until the mixture feels soft and is thick in texture. Remove the bay leaf (and the cloves if you can find them!), taste, and if felt necessary, add a little more sugar and/or vinegar until it is to your personal liking. Season with the salt and pepper – turning it thoroughly into the mixture – before placing the chutney into sterilized Kilner jars.

Apple Chutney – traditionally served with pork, but equally as good with rabbit!

Apple Chutney – Really Spicy

One of the excellent recipes kindly given to us by Mary Hart, this one is a spicy offering and should go very well with curried rabbit, for example.

50g/1¾oz medium heat curry powder
30g/1oz mustard powder
2.5kg/5½lb cooking apples, peeled, cored and diced
1.35kg/2lb10oz onions, peeled and diced
55g/2oz garlic, crushed

450g/1lb sultanas
1.5ltr/2½ pints malt vinegar
3 teaspoons all-spice berries (tied in a muslin bag and crushed)
1.5kg/3½lb Demerara sugar

Mix the curry powder and mustard with a little of the vinegar and set aside.

Place the apples, onions, garlic and sultanas in a preserving pan, together with the vinegar and spice bag. Bring to the boil, then cook gently for about an hour. Now add the sugar, stirring all the time. Cook gently until starting to thicken, and then add the curry powder/mustard mix.

Simmer until thick; then remove the spice bag. Pot into warm, sterile jars, pressing the mixture down gently in order to remove any air pockets. Cover, label and store for two months before using.

Caribbean Chutney

We just loved the idea of including something that could have come from the Caribbean in a book containing rabbit recipes, and Lynn Brodie was happy to oblige with this unique recipe.

6 medium onions
1.2ltr/2 pints malt vinegar
3kg/6½lb ripe peeled large bananas
(allow 4kg/9lb before peeling –
more if the bananas are small)
1kg/2¼lb seedless raisins
2 large Bramley cooking apples
3 level teaspoons salt
6 teaspoons medium heat curry powder

1 teaspoon medium heat chilli powder
3 yellow peppers
3 red peppers
8 large gloves garlic
3 teaspoons ground turmeric
½ teaspoon ground cloves
1.5kg/4½lb soft light brown sugar
1 packet (sachet) coconut cream

Simmer the chopped onions in vinegar until softened and opaque. Add the mashed banana, raisins and grated cooking apple and bring to the boil, simmering for a few minutes.

Remove the pan from the heat. Add the curry powder, chilli powder, chopped yellow and red peppers, crushed garlic, ground turmeric, ground cloves and salt. Slowly pour in the sugar, stirring continuously until it is dissolved.

Return the pan to the heat and stir until simmering to ensure that all the sugar dissolves into the mixture and doesn't stick. Simmer gently, reducing the chutney until thick, stirring every 10 minutes.

Remove the solid coconut cream from its clear sachet and cut into small pieces. Add this to the chutney and stir, simmering until it has dissolved completely. Continue to simmer on a very low heat for a further 30 minutes to disperse the coconut flavour (stirring every 5 minutes at this stage to avoid sticking).

Pour into hot, sterilized jars, and seal with sterile lids.

Spicy Ratatouille Chutney

Ann Lambert of Redford, West Sussex, is well known and respected amongst fellow chutney makers; she says that this recipe should make about four 450g/1lb jars, and will take about 45 minutes to prepare, plus 2 to 3 hours of cooking time. Ann also suggests that 'this is a very hot and spicy chutney – as the name implies. It may be "tamed" a little by using less cayenne pepper and paprika if you wish.'

500g/1lb 2oz onions, peeled and chopped
2 good cloves of garlic or 3 smaller ones,
peeled and crushed
500g/1lb 2oz courgettes, thinly sliced
1kg/2¼lb tomatoes – good and ripe,
skinned and chopped
2 peppers – ideally one red and one green

1 large cooking apple
1 medium-sized aubergine, finely chopped
1 tablespoon each of salt, paprika, ground
coriander and cayenne pepper
300ml/10fl oz malt vinegar
375g/13oz Demerara sugar

Put into a large pan all the ingredients except the vinegar and the sugar. Cook gently in a covered pan stirring occasionally until the juices run; boil the mixture very briefly, then simmer for about 1 to 1½ hours. Stop when all the vegetables are soft, but their shapes can still be seen.

Spicy Ratatouille Chutney.

Add the vinegar and sugar. Stir to dissolve this, and then cook gently for another hour or so. There should be no vinegar floating on the mixture, and the chutney will become quite thick.

Spoon into prepared jars. Cool, label with the name and date and…the difficult bit… wait for at least two months for it to mature!

Microwave Mango

The preparation of pickles (and chutneys) is usually based on traditional methods and utensils. There is, however, no reason why some recipes should not be done in a micro- wave. The quantities given here should fill one 450g/1lb jar. Mango Chutney is often served with rabbit.

3 mangoes, peeled and cut into small pieces   200ml/7fl oz cider vinegar

2.5cm/1in piece fresh root ginger, finely chopped   ½ level teaspoon ground ginger

1 small green chilli, seeded and finely chopped   1 garlic clove, peeled and crushed

115g/4oz soft light brown sugar

Place all the ingredients into a large bowl and microwave on 'High' for 5 minutes, or until the sugar has dissolved. Stir occasionally.

Then three-quarters cover the bowl with clingfilm and further microwave on 'High' for another 20 minutes, or until thick and well reduced; stir two or three times during cooking, and after every minute for the last 5 minutes in order to prevent the surface of the chutney from drying out.

Allow to stand for 5 minutes, then spoon into sterilized jars in the usual fashion. Cover and store for three months.

Note: Microwaves can, of course, be very useful in sterilizing jars prior to packing with chutneys, pickles and relishes. Fill clean jars one-quarter full of water and bring to a full boil. Then remove from the microwave, pour out the water and leave the jars to dry upside down on a wire rack. The jars will not all come to the boil at the same time, and – most importantly – they should *always* be removed from the microwave using oven gloves.

Herbs such as coriander have a multitude of uses, not only in the main course rabbit recipes, but also in trimmings and accompaniments.

Wine and Drinks

Not everyone drinks alcohol. Make sure that there are sufficient alternatives for those who don't – and always make sure that there is plenty of iced water, topped up with thick slices of lime for both the drinkers and non-drinkers. As a non-alcoholic drink, make several jugs of cranberry juice and sparkling water; add a few raspberries, slices of lemon and cubes of ice, and the combination is sufficient to make people feel welcome and that you've made an effort, and it's 'dry' enough not to leave a 'clawing' feeling in the mouth. Make sure that there is enough left to take to the table, because even the heavy drinkers will be trying it later!

As an alternative, make this old-fashioned non-alcoholic lemon drink: grate the rind and squeeze the juice of three lemons into a 1.5ltr/3 pint jug; add 100g/3½oz sugar, and top up with just under 1.5ltr/3 pints of boiling water. Allow it to go cold before serving, and just before you do, skim off the pieces of rind. It makes a refreshing tangy drink without spoiling the taste buds for what's to eventually come as a meal.

In the winter, greet your alcoholic guests with mulled wine or a Pimm's Winter Cup: in the summer treat them to a Pimm's No. 4, a gin and tonic, or a very, very dry Martini – all of which will entertain them happily without leaving a detrimental taste in the mouth.

The Perfect Dry Martini

A dry Martini will not affect the taste buds and spoil a later meal – it might, however, affect the heads of those who participate too freely! One of the authors went to a wedding on a Scottish island and suffered such a consequence. Ingredients are per small glass!

3 parts Bombay Sapphire gin	A twist of lemon
1 part dry vermouth	1 olive

Stir the gin and vermouth together with ice in a mixing glass. Strain into a cocktail glass, add the olive, and serve.

HOW TO SERVE WINES

Red wine should be served in clear, quite large, rounded glasses. If they are tulip-shaped they will concentrate the bouquet, very much a plus point according to the *aficionados*. Cut glass looks very well on the dining table, but unfortunately does not show off the wine to its best advantage. Temperature is important – a red is best served at about 16–18°C, although a Saumur wine or Beaujolais can be placed in the fridge for some summer time lunch drinking. Even a bottle of really good white wine can be spoiled by serving it too warm and it should be chilled in the fridge door for between one and two hours.

Open reds a short time beforehand and let them 'breathe' – even a cheap young wine is likely to benefit, and for an expensive bottle you've been looking forward to trying for ages, it is essential. If necessary, gently pour the wine from the bottle down the interior sides of a decanter, as this will allow more of the wine to come into contact with air. If there is likely to be much sediment at the bottom of the bottle, line a clean plastic funnel with a coffee filter and periodically pour a little of the wine into the decanter via the funnel.

A point of note here: although most unfinished bottles of 'ordinary' wines will keep for a couple days or more if recorked, they will not do so if left in the decanter for any length of time. Whilst it is desirable to let a red wine breathe, conversely, too much oxygen is death to opened wine and its taste will very rapidly deteriorate.

CORKSCREWS

Before you do anything to your wine, let alone drink it, it is of course necessary to open the bottle! More and more wines are being sold with screw-top caps, which, although they originally caused the wine buffs to hold up their hands in horror, are, it must be said, a 'good idea' as it means a half-full bottle (or half-empty, depending upon whether you are a pessimist or optimist!) can be kept for another day. Those that are still stopped with corks are increasingly done so with a manufactured plastic type rather than the traditional sort made from the bark of a tree – a fact that causes dismay to the producers of such cork, but is nevertheless good from the point of view of ensuring that no harmful bacteria can enter the wine because of an imperfect cork.

The choice of corkscrews is quite amazing, but the one known as a 'Waiter's Friend' is perhaps the most common. It works by lever action: once you've inserted the screw into the cork, you wedge a metal lever on to the edge of the bottle and then slowly draw the cork out. Others include the wooden double helix design, the screw-pull, and the metal double lever. Really fancy kitchen counter or wall-mounted types are available, but at a price. Before opening, cut round the foil top in such a way that when the wine is poured, it does not come into contact with the parts of the top that remain; and once the cork is drawn, it may pay to wipe round the bottle mouth with a clean napkin or paper kitchen towel in order to clear away any bits of cork or dirt.

The main reason for including this little section is, however, to suggest that the reader considers starting a corkscrew collection! It is the sort of hobby that we think will appeal to many, due to the fact that there are countless varieties out there. Some are quite ornate and extremely old and will, unfortunately, not come cheap. Others will, and once you've begun a collection, you will soon be scouring the antique shops, folly markets and car boot sales. Why not collect only those with a theme – the rabbit cook will quite likely be a shooting enthusiast, and there are corkscrews that reflect this particular interest.

WINE TO ACCOMPANY RABBIT

Bizarrely, rabbit is associated with hare (and perhaps even venison) in the public mind – if this were true, then a heavy wine would be needed, but as rabbit meat is actually more like chicken, the wines should therefore be somewhat lighter. The situation becomes slightly more complicated, however, when a heavy sauce is added to the rabbit dish or a warming winter casserole is created – in which case, a heavier wine might be beneficial.

A very knowledgeable friend of ours suggests 'any young Italian red, a Chinon, Chirou-bles, Saumur Champigny, Fleurie or even rosé from the Rhone Valley.' He also maintains that a cold rabbit pie, pâté or terrine could be accompanied by 'a white Burgundy, Cru Beaujolais, champagne or a good New Zealand chardonnay.' All of his suggestions are, it must be admitted, relatively light, but if you fancy something with a little more body (and generally a higher price), try French wines such as Côte Rôte, St Estephe or a Margaux. We personally like Italian wines with rabbit – they go well (and so they should, bearing in mind that rabbit dishes are commonplace in that country). Try a Barolo, or if you prefer a more lightweight Italian wine comparable to the French Saumur Champigny or Fleurie, a Montepulciano d'Abruzzo.

If you are looking for a Spanish wine (and again, rabbit dishes are popular in Spain), go for a Rioja, or anything from the Navarra region. Portuguese wines are also good: try one of the Dão types, or – and be really rebellious here – why not go for a white Morgado port? Aged in oak casks (as are most, if not all, fortified wines), this particular port works well with a rich recipe, as its dryness combats and compliments the sweetness of many a sauce. But serve it in small glasses; even though your guests might think you are a little mean, to use big ones would be a waste, and too much would leave them nursing hang-overs rather than fond memories of your hospitality!

With country rabbit recipes, why not try a country wine? Long before wines were made from grapes, the early Britons were drinking fruit wines. Traditionally hidden at the back of the cupboard, country wines are often treated with alarm and suspicion, and many are the tales told of horrendous sore heads brought about as a result of trying a seemingly innocu-ous pea-pod wine or similar home-made concoction. Try serving Granny's traditional wine with food, rather than as an aperitif or, worse still, after a meal that has already been accom-panied by a serious amount of alcohol. If you can get hold of a plum wine from somewhere, you will find it goes quite well with many game dishes, including rabbit.

TIPS FOR STORAGE

Traditionally, bottles of wine are always stored on their sides to ensure that the corks do not dry out, and even screw-tops are best stored this way in order to allow any sediment to settle. Always choose a dark area as your wine 'cellar', and keep bottles well away from anything that may cause the wine to become tainted as a result of an unwanted taste being introduced through the porous cork – the garden shed might be good in that it is cool, dark and undisturbed, but it would be a shame if your wine tastes of over-wintered garlic or lawn-mower petrol as a result of sharing the same space! If you have to keep your wine in a light place, cover it with a heavy blanket; wrap individual bottles in paper or, by far the simplest solution, keep them in the boxes in which they were bought.

The Domestic Rabbit

If you ask anyone where the wild rabbit originated from, most people will tell you that it was brought over by the Normans after the invasion of England by William the Conqueror. Ask them where the domesticated/table/pet rabbit originated, and nine times out of ten, they will look at you nonplussed.

A BRIEF HISTORY

The story of the rabbit as a species actually starts in the Iberian Peninsula during the Ice Ages. Why they should have evolved from there rather than anywhere else is uncertain, but the fact that they remained pretty isolated until towards the end of the last glaciations is probably due to geographical and climatic pressures. With the drastic changes in land mass brought about by this final Ice Age, they were able to colonize wider tracts and breed ... well ... like rabbits!

Research appears to show that evidence of rabbits first appearing in any domesticated form whatsoever is when the sea-faring Phoenician traders took them to North Africa some thousand years before the birth of Christ. Incidentally, and presumably of particular interest to anyone reading this book, rabbit meat would eventually become an important ingredient of North African Maghreb cuisine – itself originating from the region of the same name, and which eventually spread through Spain, Portugal, Sicily and Malta, and is the reason why so many rabbit recipes feature on the menus of numerous Mediterranean countries.

Rabbits became known to the Romans approximately a century before Christianity. Prior to that time, they had been keeping domesticated hares in large walled-in gardens known as *leporaria*, which were subsequently adapted so as to take into account the burrowing propensities of rabbits. The fact that rabbits bred in greater numbers than hares ever could, meant that they soon totally usurped hares as a provider of meat for the table. Eventually the Romans brought the rabbit (along with pheasants and fallow deer, amongst other things) to Britain, where they provided vital protein for the conquering legions. Distasteful though it undoubtedly sounds to us, the Romans apparently much enjoyed eating newborn rabbits – a trend and delicacy that once again became popular with medieval European monks who, because of the Christian edict that only fish could be consumed on Fridays and fast days, decided that, under the classification system in use at the time, foetal or newborn rabbits, being born hairless, were justifiably an aquatic species and could therefore be consumed on such days!

RABBIT WARRENS AND ISLANDS

After the departure of the Romans from Britain, originally wild but semi-domesticated rabbits went feral, but they failed to do well in the wet climate of Great Britain – they did, after all, originate in a warmer environment, and therefore thrived best in dry, sandy conditions rather than on the cold clay soil of the UK. In fact to all intents and purposes, they became extinct until they were reintroduced after the Norman Conquest of 1066, when they were originally kept in large, fenced-in areas known as warrens (or, as the French knew them, *greenness*), fed bundles of fodder, and culled for the table when required. Rabbits were not introduced to Ireland until the Normans colonized the country in the twelfth century. Kept only by wealthy landowners, the enclosed, sheltered warrens and artificial burrows offered protection and a perfect breeding environment for the rabbit, and its well-being was further assured by the employment of warreners, who looked after them and lived in specifically built homes incorporated into the warren walls.

Although by the 1500s some warrens had become so huge that they were large enough to be popular as royal hunting grounds, they nevertheless began life purely as a way of ensuring that a fresh supply of meat was always available. Henry VIII had warrens that not only provided rabbits for food, but also offered some sporting (particularly falconry) opportunities. His daughter Queen Elizabeth I kept her rabbit stocks on islands

Thetford Warren Lodge as it is now . . .

. . . and as it was before fire damage.

situated in lakes and large rivers, from which there was no opportunity for them to escape. The idea of 'rabbit' islands was eventually used by inhabitants of other countries – as can be evidenced by Coney Island in New York.

UK archaeologists have discovered some quite complex warrens, but generally, the only evidence of their existence that remains today is in place names such as Warren Hill, Warren Common and Warrener's Cottage. Even as late as 1894, according to public records, gamekeepers such as James Storey lived at a house called The Warren; whilst being responsible for the game of his employers (the Vyners of Newby Hall near Ripon, North Yorkshire), he kept '. . . a mare called "Fanny" and a cart, several dogs and ferrets. A seed and a ploughing field for hay and turnips with which to feed the rabbits in winter.' Exactly a century before, other records further show that rabbits had been imported to the estate 'some years since from a warren in Lincolnshire whither they had been brought from Ireland.'

Interestingly, for much of the time, rabbits were kept for their fur rather than their meat value – on the Thetford Chase rabbits without their skins were being sold for next to nothing in baskets by the hundredweight in the 1860s – the supposition being that the value was in their skins, which had already been sold. Not only were they sold to London furriers, but they were also exported abroad, the best paying countries being Russia and China. No wonder, then, that rabbits were so well cared for throughout the centuries. Given such protection, it was natural that the rabbit population would do well, and subsequent generations became ever more hardened to the vagaries of the British weather.

It is undoubtedly escapees from these man-made warrens, and also human interest (dating from Norman times, and including the early twentieth century), which are mainly responsible for the rabbit populating the British countryside.

SUBSEQUENT DOMESTICATION

Although semi-domesticated rabbits continued to exist in warrens, it was mainly as a result of domestication by the monastic orders, and the subsequent introduction of cage rearing, that rabbit keeping for the table evolved, certainly as we know it today. Rather than the cooks of the day just picking animals that were readily available and supplied by the warreners, specific breeds were developed; among these was the Champagne d'Argent, nowadays thought to be one of the oldest breeds of rabbit raised for its meat.

Rabbits were also bred for their fur colour and density, and the fur used to make various items of clothing and wearable accessories. Even as late as the 1920s, rabbit fur was very popular in the making of felt hats, for example, and the expression 'as mad as a hatter' is thought to have derived from the fact that chemicals used in the curing of rabbit fur for such a purpose would affect the sanity of the manufacturer.

But the rabbit remained popular as a source of meat: kept throughout the centuries as a cheap source of food, it was particularly prized by many householders during the two horrendous World Wars of the twentieth century, when it was difficult to obtain meat of any kind. At the cessation of hostilities and rationing, however, the consumption of rabbit meat dropped considerably once other types of meat became available from the local butchers. Such a change in consumer habits did not, however, stop rabbits from being kept as pets, and most people today will have kept at least one during their childhood – and even those that did not will most likely have been given a stuffed rabbit toy as a toddler, or been brought up with tales of Peter Rabbit, or watched the exploits of Thumper in the Disney cartoons. And therein lies the problem experienced by many commercial table rabbit producers: with such thoughts uppermost in the public's mind, who amongst them wants to sit down to a meal, the main ingredient of which is 'cuddly bunny'?

OVEN-READY RABBITS FOR THE TABLE

In many European countries, oven-ready rabbits are easily sourced at almost any and every supermarket, especially in France and Spain where they are as popular as chicken. Rabbit seems popular in North America, too – and has been since the mid-1980s, when some breeders began to produce a cross-bred table rabbit that was mature in a very short space of time (eight to ten weeks) and was tender enough to be fried or cooked

Warreners in the late 1890s.

by the usual methods. As a result, their commercially produced animals have a small bone structure, a lot of meat and almost no fat.

Everywhere, rabbits intended for the table must conform to the necessary human consumption standards, but even so, the UK public seem generally not to be keen on rabbit meat, as otherwise it would surely be more commonly seen in all supermarkets rather than in just a select few, as is the case at the moment. Fortunately it is available from many butchers and food markets, and orders for fresh farmed rabbit have increased significantly. It is also available by mail order from a number of suppliers, and is usually despatched and delivered overnight in an insulated box with freezer gel-packs to help maintain the product temperature.

Various terms are used to describe a particular rabbit size and likely age: for example, 'fryer' generally refers to a rabbit weighing not less than 700g/1½lb and rarely more than 1.5kg/3½lb, and less than twelve weeks of age. The flesh is tender and can be cooked in much the same way as young poultry. A 'roaster' or 'mature' rabbit may refer to an animal of any weight, but is usually over 2.5kg/4½lb, and over six months of age. The flesh is firm and coarse-grained, and may need to be slow cooked by braising or stewing, so choose your recipe accordingly.

Fresh or frozen, commercially reared rabbit meat is sold all year round and can be used in a variety of dishes.

Fresh or frozen, commercially reared rabbit meat is sold all year round, from which you can produce the most interesting of dishes.

KEEPING TABLE RABBITS

Whilst a cookery and recipe book is not the place to go into great depth regarding the rearing of rabbits for the table, the subject is nevertheless worth a brief mention, because if you can get away from the idea of rabbits being children's pets, the reality of doing so is well worth considering.

There are some excellent large breed meat rabbits that grow quickly, the most common of which is probably the New Zealand White, closely followed by the Californian. Some commercial producers have pure-bred stock of each of the two breeds, and crossbreed them to produce more vigorous young that grow more quickly. Purely because they have already been mentioned in connection with the history of the rabbit as a food source, the Champagne D'Argent is worth a name-check here. It is perhaps the oldest pure breed of rabbit and weighs about 6kg (13lb) at maturity.

Housing

Rabbit housing is minimal and takes up little space. Hutches are probably the easiest option, and you can make them yourself or buy them. Moveable arks are preferable, however, but you will need to equip them with mesh floors so that, although the inhabitants can still graze the grass protruding through, they cannot dig their way out. Such arks also provide protection against the direct weather while still allowing for a good flow of fresh air; as with all livestock keeping, adequate ventilation is vital for healthy rabbits. Several hutches or arks will be needed when breeding in order to house adult does, youngsters and a resting buck.

Breeding

When a doe is to be mated it is a simple matter of putting her with the buck (do it the other way round and it is not unusual for the doe to fight and even kill the buck). Females are ready to mate at around five months, but they can become pregnant much earlier, so be aware of this possibility when keeping youngsters of both sexes mixed together.

Unusually, rabbits do not have to come into season before being mated; it is good practice to leave them together for at least twenty-four hours so that you can be reasonably sure that the buck has mated with the doe at least two or three times (technically, the doe ovulates in response to the buck's presence). Outdoors she will breed during spring and summer, but if housed indoors she can breed throughout the year.

Gestation takes thirty-one days, and a day or so before she is due, the doe will start gathering bedding together to make a nest, and will pull out some of the fur from her breast with which to line it. Young rabbits can be weaned at eight weeks, when the best practice is to remove the doe and put her in another hutch, thereby leaving the youngsters in familiar surroundings – by which time the young of some breeds will already be 'market ready', weighing 2kg (4½lb).

Feeding

Young rabbits will wean themselves by nibbling at their mother's solid food. Whatever food is used for adult stock, ensure that it contains the correct balance of protein, fats, fibre, carbohydrates, minerals and vitamins; but remember that some rabbit foods also contain additives such as coccidiostats and probiotics, which are not necessarily good things to be included in the diet of an animal that is eventually going to end up in the human food chain. The best way to tell if your rabbit is getting enough feed is to stroke its backbone regularly: if the bumps of its backbone feel sharp and pointed, increase its feed; if you can feel the bumps but they feel rounded, you are giving the right amount; if you feel no bumps at all, then decrease your rabbit's intake.

IN CONCLUSION

It might seem somewhat insensitive to jump straight from rearing rabbits to considering treating them as a meat commodity. However, the fact remains that the rabbit, whether wild or domesticated, can provide an easily accessible meat source – and when considering it as such, rather than as a 'pet', is it any different to the way we consider gambolling lambs in the spring, and yet conveniently forget that they are one and the same when you buy 'spring lamb' from your local butcher? They have, as we have seen, been a major part of protein nutrition when otherwise things might have proved tough, and they have been the target of sporting enthusiasts throughout the ages. And despite everything that's been against them over the centuries, they have survived – and will continue to do so for generations to come.

The Ancient House Museum's reconstruction of a Victorian kitchen table preparing for the making of a rabbit pie.

Glossary

al dente   Vegetables or, more commonly, pasta, cooked, but firm to the bite.

allspice   Dried berry of the pimento tree of the clove family.

allumette   Vegetables, potatoes or other items cut into the size and shape of matchsticks.

arroser   To sprinkle with liquid, or to baste.

bain marie   A deep container, half-filled with water in which other cooking pots are placed in order to cook gently in the oven. Usually used for terrines and similar dishes. A shop-bought *bain marie* is traditionally a wide, cylindrical metal container made of at least two basic parts – an outer container that holds water and an inner, smaller container that fits inside the outer one and which holds the material to be heated or cooked. Typically the inner container is immersed about halfway into the water. The smaller container, filled with the substance to be heated, fits inside and the whole is heated in the oven at, or below, the base, causing the temperature of the materials in both containers to rise as needed. The insulating action of the water helps to keep the contents of the inner pot from boiling or scorching.

bard   Place slices of bacon over rabbit meat to prevent it from drying out when roasting.

baste   Regularly spoon over the roasting meat some of the fat or liquid in which it is cooking.

beurre manié   A mixture, by equal parts of flour and butter, used to thicken sauces. *See also* roux.

black pepper   Immature berries (white pepper is the mature berries with the hull removed).

blanch   A cooking technique of placing food into boiling water for a short time, then in cold water to stop cooking.

bouillon   Unclarified stock or broth from meat.

bouquet garni   Sprig of thyme, parsley and bay leaf, tied together and used to flavour stews and casseroles.

braising   A combination of roasting and stewing; usually used on tougher joints of meat.

broil   Method of cooking to describe grilling a dish in the bottom of a grill pan when other ingredients and liquid mixes have been added.

cassoulet   A casserole of stewed meat and beans.

caul fat   The lining of a pig's stomach – used to protect the food within as it is being roasted.

Cayenne Powdered red pepper.

celeriac The root of a variety of celery, used raw or cooked in a variety of rabbit recipes.

chervil A mild, aniseed-flavoured herb related to parsley.

chilli peppers Many varieties from mild to hot.

clarified butter Butter cleared of impurities by melting slowly and removing the unwanted liquid that forms at the base.

concasser To chop roughly or pound in a mortar.

confit Generally 'confit' is used to describe meat preserved in duck fat, but occasionally it is used as a cooking term to indicate a method whereby fat is heated in a pan, the meat (or sometimes fish such as salmon) is added and submerged until tender and then used immediately (but after being allowed to rest for a short while).

coriander seed Used whole or in coarse or fine powder form. This herb is of the carrot family and has the flavour of sage and lemon peel. When stocking your pantry get both the seeds and the powder.

cropinette A word French in origin, used to describe caul fat.

croûton Small cube of fried or toasted bread served as a garnish to soup or alongside certain pigeon dishes.

dariole mould Looks like a small metal cup. Its shape is cylindrical with a slight taper to it, and it may or may not have a lip around the top. Anodized aluminium is often used for dariole moulds, as this metal is said to help food lift out easily as well as brown evenly. Darioles vary in size, but are always quite small as they are meant to be for individual portions of food.

deglaze To loosen meat residue in a pan or roasting dish after roasting or frying with a wooden spoon and adding wine or stock in order to make gravy.

dice To cut food into small cubes of about 5mm (¼ in) across.

duxelle A purée of very finely chopped mushrooms, sweated in butter, with a little chopped onion, which can then be used for stuffing rabbit, or as a sauce base.

earthenware Cooking pot made of fired clay.

émonder To skin tomatoes, peppers and suchlike, by plunging them into boiling water for a few seconds and then dipping them into cold water.

étouffé A cooking method similar to braising in which items are cooked with little or no added liquid in a pan with a tight-fitting lid.

farina Flour or meal made of cereal, nuts, or starchy roots.

farrago Medley or mixture of foodstuffs.

filo (pastry) A type of leaved pastry.

fines herbes A mixture of finely chopped herbs, traditionally chervil, chives, parsley and tarragon.

fumet In cooking, the juices that have run from meat during cooking – elsewhere it is a name for deer droppings!

garam masala Adds flavour and fragrance to Indian dishes, including chutneys and pickles. It is a combination of various whole spices. You can buy it ready-made in the stores or make your own.

garnish To decorate food dishes, especially just before serving.

glug A glug (or two) of oil or wine is often referred to by modern chefs – although a very loose measurement, it is described thus: put your thumb over the top of the bottle and tip it up. When you let your thumb off, the liquid will glug once, or twice (as required) as it comes out.

gremolata Very finely chopped lemon zest, juice and parsley.

infuse To steep herbs or similar in liquid in order to extract the flavoursome content.

julienne Vegetables cut into short, thin strips.

larding A method whereby thin strips of fat are pushed through meat in order to prevent it from drying out during cooking.

lardons Small squares of bacon or pork belly fat.

legumes Any member of the pea family, including chick peas, runner beans, soya beans and lentils.

mandolin Not in this instance a musical instrument, but a slicer used to produce julienne vegetables.

marinade A liquid and/or herb mix in which meat and game is left for several hours. *See also* marinate.

marinate To add liquid or dry ingridients (or a mixture of the two, such as wine and herbs) to meat or fish in order to impart flavour or to tenderize.

medallions Small rounds of meat.

mirepoix Coarsely diced vegetables.

mixed spice Classically, a mixture containing caraway, allspice, coriander, cumin, nutmeg and ginger.

papillote Greaseproof paper or kitchen foil forming a casing around food in order that meat can self-baste whilst roasting.

parboil To partially cook food by boiling briefly in water.

peppercorns Most often used whole. If required in powdered form, they taste best when freshly ground.

pinch An approximate measure of any ingredient, but usually an amount held between thumb and forefinger.

quenelles Technically, a lightly poached dumpling based on a mixture or combination of chicken and/or rabbit bound with eggs and shaped into an oval by the use of two spoons, but used generally to describe the method of serving mashed potatoes and/or vegetables.

ragoût Meat stewed with vegetables and highly seasoned.

reduce To reduce a liquid-based mixture by boiling until it thickens to the desired consistency.

refresh Most commonly used in reference to blanched vegetables that are placed immediately in iced water to stop the cooking, set the colour and restore the crispness. Greens and herbs that are still very fresh, but have gone limp, can be restored to their original state by placing in cold water and then patted dry.

roux A mixture of fat and flour used in sauces.

sauté Rapid cooking in oil, usually in a heavy-bottomed sauce or frying pan.

searing To quickly brown meat at a high temperature in order to retain its juices.

spice bag Home-made muslin bag used to hold spices in order that they might add flavour to a cooking dish without leaving a bitter taste.

suer *See sweat.*

sweat Cooking vegetables very slowly in butter or oil so as to draw out the moisture and soften them. Care must be taken that the fat does not become too hot and brown, otherwise the vegetables will just remain raw and burn.

translucent Cooking (onions, for example) until clear or transparent.

trivet A metal rack placed over, or in, a roasting tin to keep the meat from sitting in its own juices.

trussing A method of holding game or meat together by tying with string and the aid of a skewer.

whisk Utensil for whisking, or the action of whipping or mixing eggs, cream, with a brisk sweeping movement. Usually necessary in recipes where air needs to be added, such as in the making of soufflés.

wine vinegar Vinegar made from wine as opposed to malt.

wood grilling By barbecuing over charcoal, the wood imparts a distinctive and unique flavour to the meat.

zest Scraping of orange, lemon or lime peel used as flavouring.

'At-a-Glance' List of Recipes

This is a general list of recipes directly appertaining to *The Rabbit Cook* – their actual page placing can be seen by referring to the index, but the point in including this additional list is to answer, at a glance, the nagging question of how best to deal with a rabbit from the field – either as a gift from a country friend, or in response to 'I saw a rabbit in the butcher's and nearly bought it, but had no idea what to do with it.'

No matter how tasty the main dish might be, it can rarely be eaten on its own: therefore also included at the end of this somewhat random list are the accompaniments suggestions – which have been carefully selected to ensure that they go perfectly with the main course.

Chicken and Rabbit Casserole

Kinga McArdle's Hungarian Rabbit and Dumpling Recipe

Curried Rabbit

Braised Rabbit Joints

Mumbled Rabbit

Slow-Cooked Rabbit with White Bean Mash and Roast Vegetables

Stuffed Roast Rabbit

Assiette of Rabbit – Rack, Saddle of Rabbit, Confit of Leg Spring Roll, Sautéed Kidneys and Rabbit Liver Parfait

Mustard Rabbit with Butternut Squash and Pumpkin

Wild Rabbit with Wild Sorrel

Devilled Rabbit

Naan Rabbit Pockets

Pish-Pash Rabbit

Marinated Rabbit

Roast Saddle of Rabbit with Braised Leg Faggot, Cannelloni Beans, Grain Mustard Spinach Ragoût and Roast Root Vegetables

Spiced Rabbit and Wholegrain Spaghetti

Congilio Ischitano

Rabbit Brawn

Blackfriars Game Terrine

Rising Sun Rabbit Terrine

Rabbit, Game and Mushroom Loaf

Wild Rabbit in Herb Mousse with Fondant Potato; Leg Ballotine and Wild Mushrooms

Rabbit in Peanut Sauce

Rabbit Goulash

Pan-Fried Rabbit Fillet with Slow Casserole of Leg Meat

Stuffed, Apricot-Glazed Leg of Rabbit

Wild Rabbit Soup

South American Rabbit Stew (*Cazuela*)

Peppers stuffed with Rabbit

Rabbit Stew with Olives

James Rogers' Rabbit Pie

Rabbit Pudding

Lawrence and Julia
   Murphy's Rabbit Pie;
   Roasted Loins and
   Cider Velouté
Dorset Rabbit
The Rising Sun Rabbit Pie
Lapin en Cidre
Rabbit with Prunes and
   Mustard
Rabbit with Prunes and
   Raisins

Vendée Rabbit with
   Shallots and
   Mushrooms
Potato and Rabbit
   Lemon-flavoured
   Dauphinoise
Rabbit and Bacon
   Pudding
Greek Traditional Rabbit
   Stew (Stifado)
Rillettes Ménagère

Barbecued Rabbit with
   Saffron and Yoghurt
Philip's Paella Valenciana
   with Rabbit
Quick Rabbit Liver Pâté
Rabbit Liver and Rocket
   Bruschetta
Rabbit in Champagne
'Fryer' rabbit
Pressure-Cooked
   Blanquette of Rabbit

'AT A GLANCE' ACCOMPANIMENT RECIPES

Roasted Ratatouille
Roasted Shallots and
   Squash
Parsnip and Apple Mash
Parsnips in Batter
Turnip and Tarragon
   Rosti
Rondle Wood Rosti
Bubble and Squeak
Spring Onion Potato
   Cakes
Pommes Boulangères
Bacon and Brussels
   Sprouts
Game Chips
Fennel and Borlotti Bean
   Bake

Cheese Potato Bakes
Seared Chanterelle
   Mushrooms
Cheesy Artichokes
Vegetable Soufflé
Mushroom and Green
   Bean Risotto
Nockerl (Hungarian
   Dumplings)
Bread Dumplings
Bread Mushroom
   Dumplings
Cheesy Nettle Potato
   Dumplings
Anchovy Stuffing
Simple Olive and Bread
   Stuffing

Spinach and Mushroom
   Stuffing
Apple Stuffing
Chestnut Purée
Game and Brown Stock
Char-Grilled Vegetable
   Quinoa Salad
Chicory and Bacon Salad
Beetroot and Red Onion
   Salad
Italian Salad
Arabian Salad
Pear and Apple Chutney
Apple Chutney
Caribbean Chutney
Spicy Ratatouille Chutney
Microwave Mango

Index

Entries in *italics* denote actual recipes